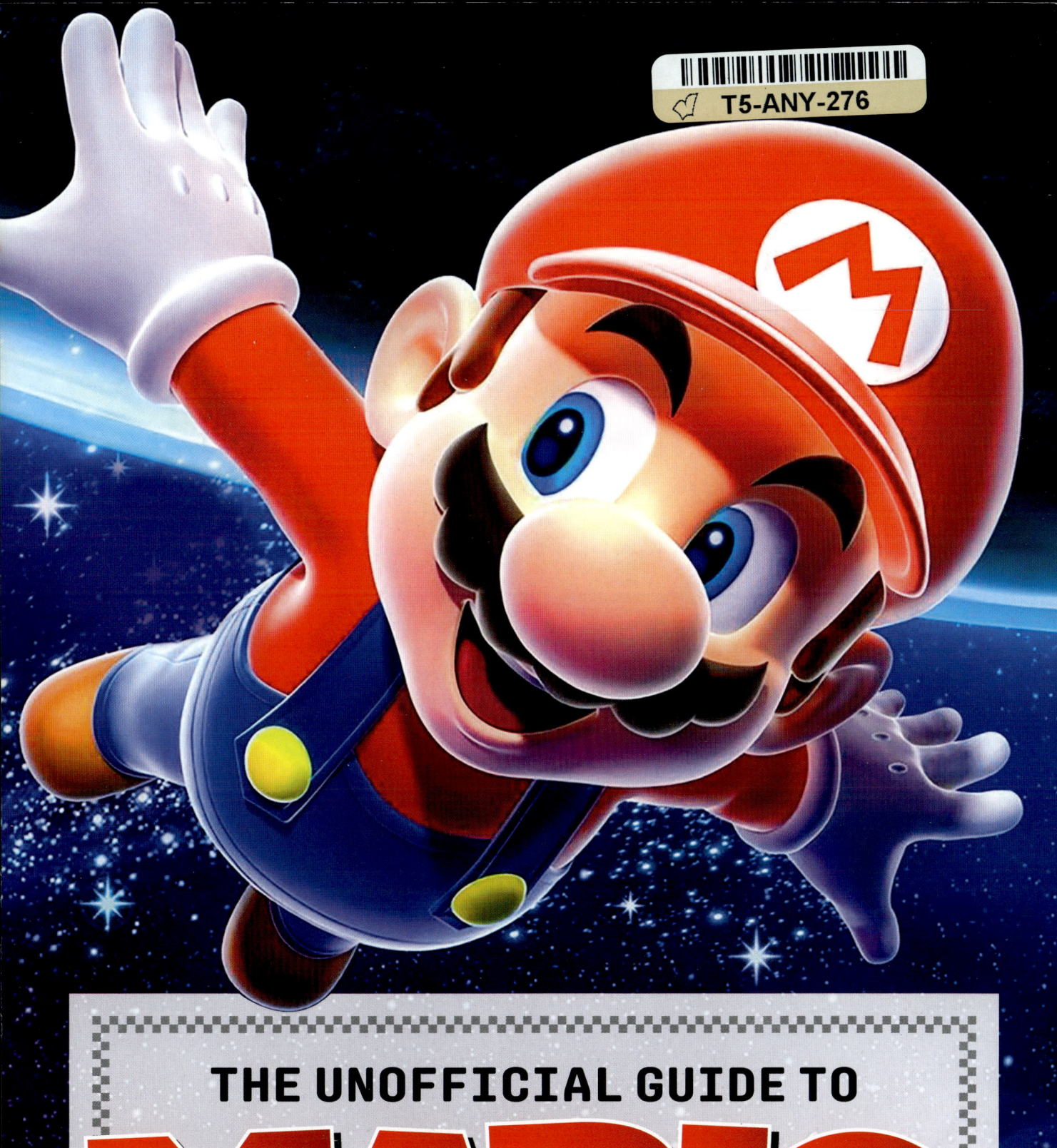

THE UNOFFICIAL GUIDE TO MARIO

INTRODUCTION

IT'S MARIO'S WORLD

We're just living in it.

As the face of over 200 video games, Mario is easily the most popular character in the Nintendo universe. Since his first appearance in 1981's *Donkey Kong*, this brave hero has helped sell over 620 million copies of games around the world and grossed more than $30 billion. Not bad for a Brooklyn plumber!

In the pages that follow, we'll reveal all of Mario's secrets and more. From his humble origins to his TV shows and Hollywood films, across seven video game consoles and even into his own amusement parks, we've got everything you want to know about Mario and his adventures with Luigi, Peach, Yoshi and the rest of the gang. So, what are you waiting for? "Let's-a go!"

CONTENTS

PART 1
MEET THE CREW

6 | Mario
Get the lowdown on the main guy, plus all his friends and his games' supporting cast of characters.

16 | Villains
These fierce foes keep Mario on his toes!

18 | The Babies
These pint-size characters sure do add big fun!

PART 2
VIDEO GAMES

22 | Mario Explained
Learn the basics about the main series.

24 | The Nintendo Entertainment System
This NES trilogy started a video game revolution.

28 | The Super Nintendo Entertainment System (SNES)
New hardware allows *Mario* to branch out like never before!

32 | Mario Kart
The fun revs up with a thrilling racing theme.

36 | The Nintendo 64 & Super Mario 64
Jumpman jumps to the third dimension.

40 | The GameCube
Good gaming leads the way for new *Mario* titles.

44 | Super Smash Bros.
Mario throws down with other popular Nintendo characters.

48 | On the Wii
New technology breathes new life into everyone's favorite plumber.

52 | Mario Sports
Our adventurous crew become athletic legends.

54 | Super Mario Odyssey
The most expansive game in the series is released.

56 | Top 10 Titles
These *Mario* hits are the best of all time!

PART 3
MEDIA EMPIRE

62 | A New Jump to the Big Screen
Dive into the hype over *The Super Mario Bros. Movie*.

66 | Super Show
The short-lived TV series becomes a cult classic.

68 | The Sounds of Success
The magical music of the popular franchise.

70 | An A-List Plumber
Hollywood can't get enough of *Mario*!

72 | Welcome to Super Nintendo World
Live your *Mario* fantasies with incredible rides and awesome attractions.

76 | Trivia Time
Test your knowledge with this fun quiz.

This publication is editorially independent and has not been licensed or approved by the owners of the characters or entertainment properties.

| PART 1 |

MEET THE CREW

A real who's who of the Mushroom Kingdom.

Learn all about (clockwise from top) Bowser, Toad, Luigi, Mario, Peach, Yoshi and the rest of the Marioverse.

MEET THE CREW

In *Super Smash Bros.* (shown here), Mario is endowed with the power of the fire flower permanently, making him even more formidable.

FIRE FLOWER

SUPER STAR

MARIO

His mission, his actions and his killer fashion.

BY NOAH PETRILLO

Mario truly is a monolith of a modern hero. Everyone loves a good underdog story, and Mario exemplifies that archetype perfectly. As confirmed by Nintendo.com, Mario is a humble Brooklyn plumber by profession but is considered by the official site as "a jack of all trades." We see so much of Mario's heroics, but hear surprisingly little from the man himself outside of his portrayal in film and on TV.

Mario, and therefore his games, hardly stand on ceremony or utilize monologues. Instead, we mainly hear the hero grunt or yell out one of his catchphrases. These include an introduction with his signature Italian accent, "It's-a me, Mario!" The majority of his lines are shouts like "Wahoo!" "Mamma mia!" and "Let's-a go!"

Perhaps Mario's strongest trait, other than his cheerful attitude and willingness to help, is his remarkable agility and jump height. The majority of *Mario* games entail running across maps while dodging various enemies and jumping on and over obstacles like spikes, moving planks and more. Mario doesn't have to rely on his agility alone, though. Along his many journeys, he encounters all sorts of helpful friends and items.

Power-Ups Aplenty

Here are some of the most popular and most common power-ups, complete with Mario's corresponding outfits!

- **Fire Flower** When Mario encounters this exotic-looking plant, he is given the ability to shoot fireballs that destroy his enemies. The plant gives Mario a snazzy color change to his outfit, switching to a red and white version of his classic overalls and hat.
- **Super Mushroom** While this power-up doesn't change Mario's outfit, it does allow him to grow into a giant! One of the most iconic power-ups in all of gaming, and considered by *Game Rant* to be his most popular power-up, the super mushroom allows Mario to take extra hits from enemies as well as destroy blocks with ease.
- **Super Star** This powerful, yellow smiling star temporarily covers Mario's clothes and skin in a rainbow. For a short time, Mario is invincible, and simply touching an enemy will destroy them.
- **Super Leaf** This striped leaf with eyes allows Mario to transform into "Tanooki Mario." Based on the *tanuki*, or Japanese raccoon dog, this adorable outfit grants Mario the ability to fly, glide and attack enemies by spinning his tail and even sometimes turn into a statue to become immune to enemies.
- **Hammer Suit** This power-up allows Mario to don essentially the same outfit as the Hammer Bros., one of many types of Koopa enemies to encounter. When wearing the suit, "Hammer Mario" is able to throw a series of hammers in a repeating arc that can be used to defeat anything.

Kingdoms and Clothing

Despite the fact that the setting of all *Mario* games is considered by many fans to be the Mushroom Kingdom, the locations actually span a wide number of kingdoms. In the earliest games, these backstories were included in the games' instruction booklets. The Game Boy game *Super Mario Land*, for example, takes place in a world called Sarasaland, an empire made up of four kingdoms.

Surprisingly, Mario's design has changed very little since his first appearance in 1981. As time has passed, Mario has gotten much more defined with the steady improvements in graphics. However, his classic outfit (blue overalls, red shirt and red hat) has been his default attire since the very beginning. It's how most people know and recognize him, but that doesn't mean he hasn't worn some other incredible outfits throughout his many adventures.

In the 1990 puzzle game *Dr. Mario*, we see our hero in a white lab coat complete with a stethoscope and head mirror. He even throws pills! The more recent game *Super Mario Odyssey* went no-holds-barred with Mario's outfits, with numerous options ranging from a bathing suit to a white tuxedo and top hat. No matter what he's wearing, Mario is one of the more fashionable heroes of modern times. ∎

Aside from power-ups, Mario has friends like Yoshi to assist him when he needs it most.

SUPER LEAF

MEET THE CREW

LUIGI

A real leading sidekick.

Here's Luigi's famous "death stare" in *Mario Kart 8*. You wouldn't like him when he's angry!

Ever wondered why so many *Mario* games have "Bros." in the title? Luigi is why. In the 2013 live presentation Nintendo Direct, the late Nintendo CEO Satoru Iwata confirmed Mario and Luigi are fraternal twins. Luigi's full name was revealed as "Luigi Mario" in the 1993 film *Super Mario Bros.*, which would make Mario "Mario Mario" (this was somewhat discredited by creator Shigeru Miyamoto).

Luigi has been around since the original *Mario Bros.* arcade game as player two. True fans know Luigi is just as heroic and capable as Mario himself. Players rejoiced when Luigi got the chance to take center stage in *Luigi's Mansion*, one of GameCube's first-ever recipients of a Player's Choice release.

In a trailer for *Mario Kart 8*, Luigi is shown passing a racer with an uncharacteristically stern look on his face. The expression came to be known as the "Luigi Death Stare," and various takes on the clip have garnered millions of views across social media.

8 THE UNOFFICIAL GUIDE TO MARIO

For more info on Peach's role in the 2023 film, see page 63.

Always displaying her unmistakably unique fashion, Peach simply can't help but dazzle everyone lucky enough to see her.

PEACH

More than just a damsel in distress.

Playing as Peach is a great choice in any *Mario Kart* game!

Peach first appeared in *Super Mario Bros.*, Mario's first major console game. In the instruction booklet, she is referred to as Princess Toadstool, which is actually her last name. Her castle in Mushroom Kingdom, over which she presides, was invaded by Koopas, and Bowser captures her to prevent her from using a spell that has the power to undo his curse on the Mushroom people.

Peach was playable as early as *Super Mario Bros. 2*, which goes to show that she's far more than someone who just needs rescuing. She eventually starred in her very own game, Nintendo DS's *Super Princess Peach*. While it has been argued over the years that Mario is in love with Princess Peach, she's never really returned the affection, seeing Mario as a dear friend. With her fierce fashion and independence, Peach Toadstool is a graceful yet mighty princess warrior we can all look up to.

Mario will always be there to help Peach when she needs it.

MEET THE CREW

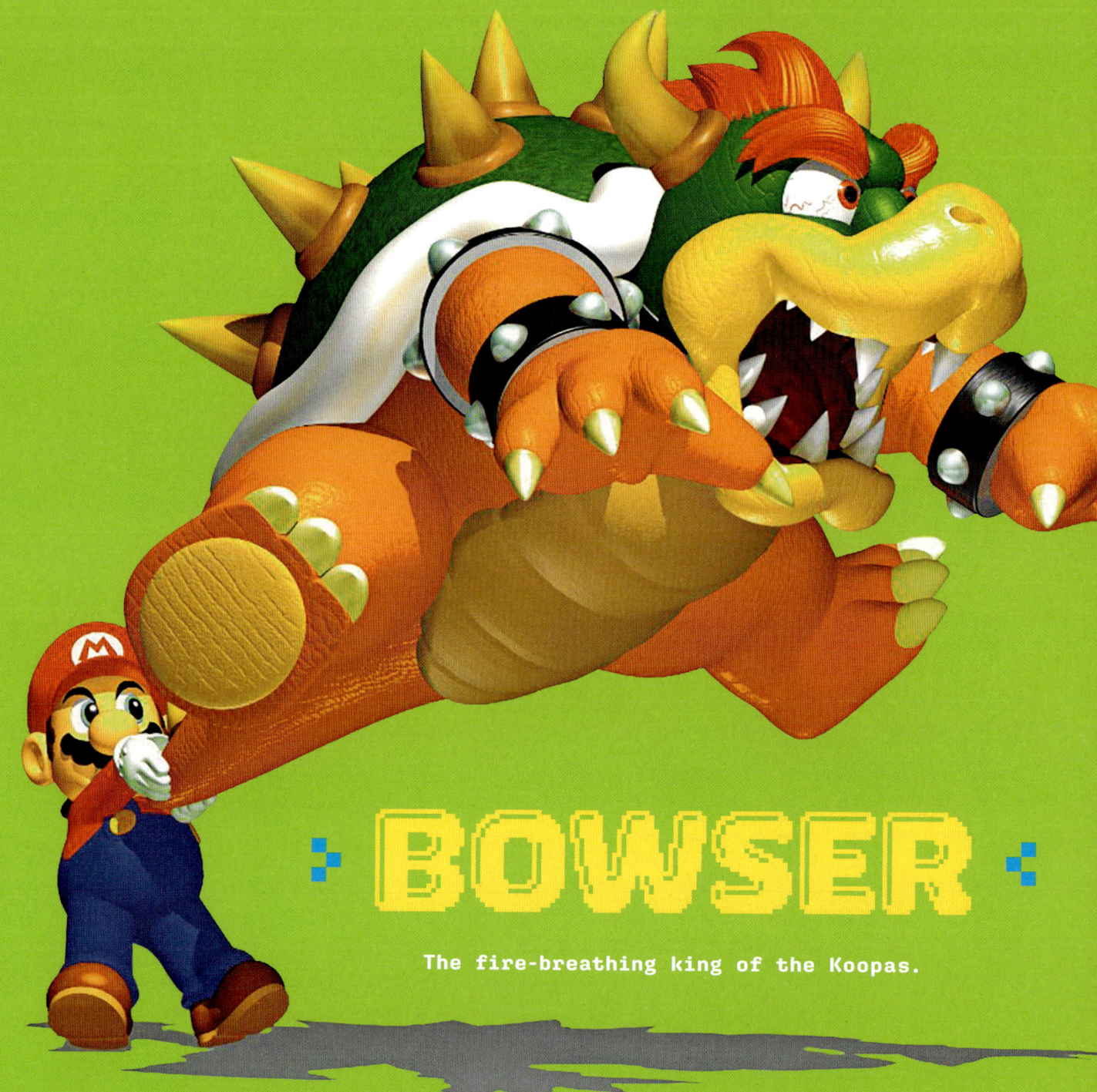

BOWSER

The fire-breathing king of the Koopas.

It's not too often that a villain is as memorable as the hero, but Bowser is undoubtedly one of those cases. It's really no wonder *Game Rant* named him the best video game villain of all time. Even beyond video games, few evildoers can compare with Bowser's longevity, iconic design and fearsome plots of domination.

Bowser has been the archnemesis of Mario since his first appearance in the original *Super Mario Bros*. As the king of the Koopa Troop, a tribe of turtlelike beings, Bowser leads his army in an assault on the Mushroom Kingdom. He puts a spell on the Mushroom people, turning them into inanimate objects, and he most often will capture Princess Peach in order to stop her intervention in his schemes. Still, he's no match for the diverse and acrobatic talents of Mario.

An Unlikely Hero
Bowser most commonly fills the role of the dastardly villain, but the more you see of him, the more complex a character he becomes.

In *Super Mario Bros. 3* (above), in World 8, Bowser gives Mario all he's got, as per usual, using his fearsome fire-wielding abilities as well as his advantage on the difficult terrain.

When Bowser's not enacting one of his diabolical schemes, his many children keep him plenty busy.

In *Super Mario RPG: Legend of the Seven Stars*, Mario and Bowser must put aside their differences to defeat a larger enemy. Bowser is also a caring father, as showcased in *Mario + Rabbids Sparks of Hope*, where Bowser Jr. is shown having to confirm with his father that he has, in fact, done his homework and taken out the trash. In *Super Mario Odyssey*, it's revealed that Bowser has romantic feelings for Princess Peach, going to great lengths to set up an incredibly elaborate wedding. He's even the hero of the sports game *Mario Golf: Super Rush*, wherein he simply wants to unfreeze the land of his people.

11

MEET THE CREW

While Toad is not always playable, if you ever find yourself in a bind, count on him to help you out with a tip or hint.

TOAD

A little assistant who never stops helping.

Recognized by the official Nintendo website as an aide to Princess Peach, Toad is constantly working for her benefit as well as the kingdom's. He joins Mario on many adventures as a guide with sage advice, and he was first featured as a playable character in *Super Mario Bros. 2*. Today, you can mostly play as Toad in the arcade-style sports and racing games like *Mario Kart*.

Like many *Mario* characters, he has a voice composed mostly of chirps and yells, while his dialogue is shown in text. Toad does, however, have a speaking voice of his own in the 2023 film. In Japan, the cute and helpful character is known as Kinopio, which is also the name of the species as a whole. Despite starting out as simply one of many nearly identical creatures, Toad has really come into his own.

12 THE UNOFFICIAL GUIDE TO MARIO

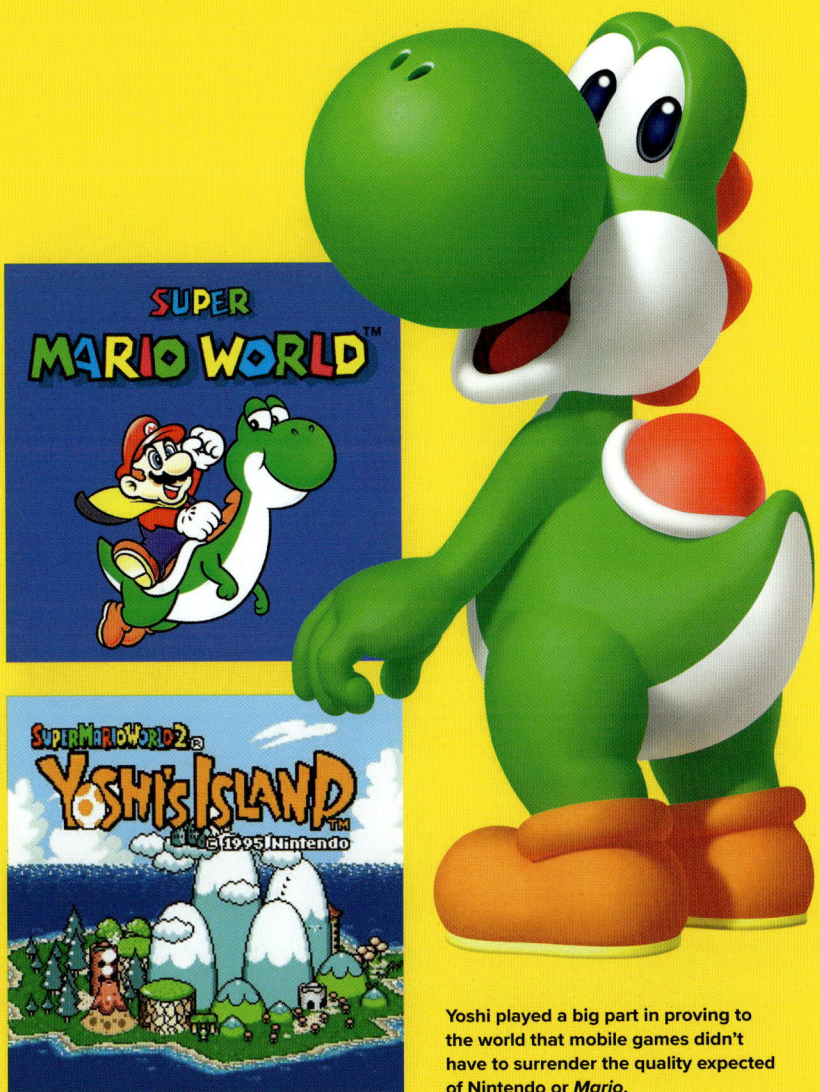

Yoshi played a big part in proving to the world that mobile games didn't have to surrender the quality expected of Nintendo or *Mario*.

YOSHI

The adorable dinosaur that rides like a horse.

Voted the No. 1 favorite character in the *Mario* universe by *TheTopTens*, Yoshi is an adorable dinosaur with quite useful special abilities. He first appeared in 1990's *Super Mario World* as Mario and Luigi's lovable sidekick you can ride like a horse.

In the sequel to Yoshi's debut game, *Super Mario World 2: Yoshi's Island*, it is revealed that Yoshi, like Toad, is one of a whole species of the same name. It's also revealed that the bond Mario and Luigi have with Yoshi stems back to when the brothers were just babies and many Yoshis came together to reunite baby Mario and baby Luigi.

Since then, Yoshi has starred in numerous spinoffs of his own in addition to being playable in the many *Mario* racing, sports and fighting games.

TOADETTE & BIRDO

Toadette first appeared as a counterpart to Toad in *Mario Kart: Double Dash!!* As this game is reliant on equal pairs of racers, creating a signature female counterpart to Toad seemed a perfect chance to add to the list of great *Mario* characters. She has since appeared in subsequent *Mario Kart* games and *Mario Golf: Super Rush*.

Birdo (though she prefers Birdetta or Birdie) was first seen in the American release of *Super Mario Bros. 2*. As the true sequel only released in Japan, Birdo, known then as Catherine, was an enemy character rumored to be caught between the two games. Since *Mario Tennis 2000*, she's largely seen as Yoshi's gaming partner.

MEET THE CREW

DAISY

An empress with endless skills.

More of an empress than a princess, Daisy first appeared in the Game Boy game *Super Mario Land*. The setting of this game, Sarasaland, is composed of four distinct kingdoms: Birabuto, Muda, Easton and Chai. Daisy rules over all four kingdoms until a dark cloud descends and the villainous Tatanga aims to marry Daisy and assume control over all four kingdoms. While there is a distinct trend in *Mario* of villains capturing princesses, Daisy is no stranger to combat. Regarded as a bit of a tomboy, you can find her playing sports with Mario and Luigi. She's also a popular choice in the arcade fighting game *Super Smash Bros. Ultimate*, where she boasts a powerful hip-check move.

ROSALINA

An intrepid yet timid galactic explorer.

A galactic traveler with a magic wand, Rosalina is the adoptive mother of the starlike creatures called Lumas. First seen in *Super Mario Galaxy*, Rosalina commands the Comet Observatory and watches the cosmos. She is considered mysterious and reserved, though she is also known for her generosity and kindness.

THE UNOFFICIAL GUIDE TO MARIO

WARIO

A rip-riding villain.

First appearing as the main antagonist and final boss of *Super Mario Land 2: 6 Golden Coins*, Wario is a purposeful polar opposite of Mario, with his name stemming from simply turning the "M" in Mario upside down. In Japanese, his name is also a play on the word *warui*, meaning "bad." While Wario considers himself Mario's archrival, that supposition adds to the comedy of his character, as both Mario and the rest of the world generally consider Bowser to be Mario's true rival.

WALUIGI

A lanky dude with an edge.

Close friend of Wario, Waluigi is bent on besting Mario and Luigi, though why he's so committed is not clear. This just adds to the silliness of him and his partner in crime and mayhem. Waluigi first appeared in *Mario Tennis* so that Wario could have a dedicated doubles partner. The rest was history, because from that point on, the two are almost always seen together.

MEET THE CREW

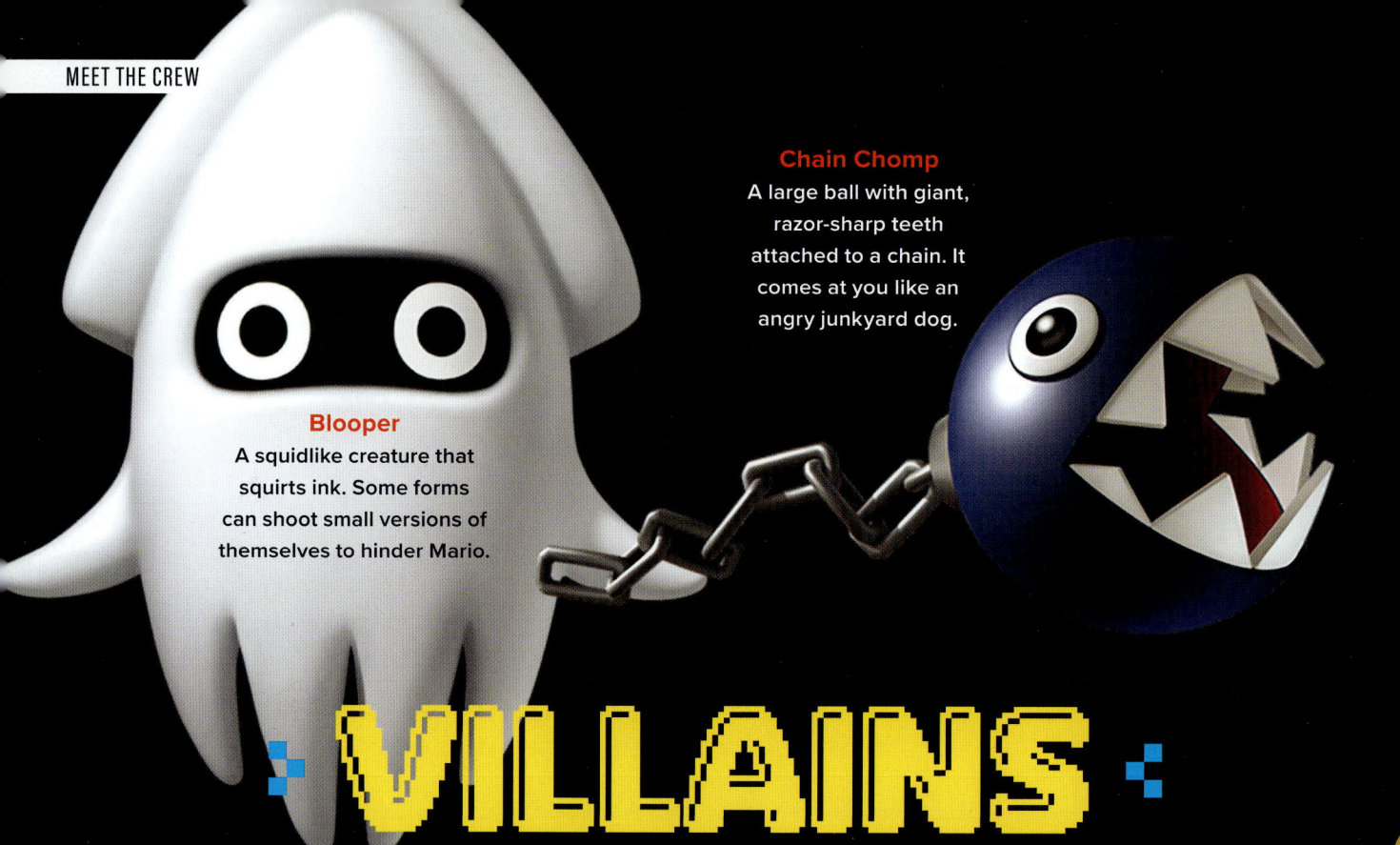

Blooper
A squidlike creature that squirts ink. Some forms can shoot small versions of themselves to hinder Mario.

Chain Chomp
A large ball with giant, razor-sharp teeth attached to a chain. It comes at you like an angry junkyard dog.

VILLAINS

These fierce foes keep Mario on his toes.

Koopa Troopas
Varying in colors and abilities, the Troopas retreat into their shells when hit, which allows them to slide around, continuing to cause damage if not picked up and thrown.

Piranha Plant
Often living in the green pipes seen throughout the games, these carnivorous plants are ready to snatch you up if you get too close.

Thwomp
These big stone blocks have scary faces and make a habit of plummeting to the ground, threatening to crush anyone who stands beneath them.

16   THE UNOFFICIAL GUIDE TO MARIO

Boo
A spherical ghost that can sneak up behind Mario if he's not careful. They are led by the fearsome and playable King Boo.

Wiggler
This adorable caterpillar is friendly until you step on or otherwise mess with it. Then, it'll turn red and charge.

Goomba
Sentient, mushroomlike creatures that roam around the Mushroom Kingdom. Mario can jump on them to defeat them.

Bob-omb
These wind-up explosives are deceptively cute.

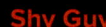

Shy Guy
Appearing ever since the American version of *Super Mario Bros. 2*, these little guys wear masks to hide their faces (because they're shy).

Cheep Cheep
A round, generally red fish that is known to leap from the water. Some even have spikes.

Lakitu
This Koopa rides on a cloud, often dropping objects from the sky to stop Mario. In the *Mario Kart* series, Lakitu holds the starting lights and picks you up if you fall off the racecourse.

MEET THE CREW

THE BABIES

These pint-size versions of main characters bring big fun!

Baby Rosalina
Debuted as a racer in *Mario Kart 8*.

Baby Mario & Baby Luigi
These tiny versions of Mario and Luigi first appeared in *Super Mario World 2: Yoshi's Island*. Seeing the famous fighting duo as infants struck a chord with players, and subsequent baby versions of other main characters have since appeared in later games.

FLASHBACK BABIES

Baby Daisy
First appeared in *Mario Kart Wii*.

Baby Donkey Kong
Featured in *Yoshi's Island DS* for Nintendo DS.

Baby Bowser
First seen in *Super Mario World 2: Yoshi's Island*. Cared for by Kamek.

Baby Peach
First featured in *Mario & Luigi: Partners in Time*.

Lumas
These star creatures come in many colors. Rosalina is their adoptive mother.

Diddy Kong
The nephew of the big gorilla goes way back to the *Donkey Kong 2* arcade game released in 1982, but Diddy was first named in 1994's *Donkey Kong Country*.

CURRENT BABIES

Bowser Jr.
Debuting in *Super Mario Sunshine*, it was teased that Bowser Jr.'s mother was Peach Toadstool! Though debunked, the theory has circulated ever since.

IGGY KOOPA
LEMMY KOOPA
ROY KOOPA
MORTON KOOPA JR.
LARRY KOOPA
LUDWIG VON KOOPA
WENDY O. KOOPA

The Koopalings (Bowser's adoptive children)
Designed and named after various musicians, these seven kids cause all kinds of trouble.

The Nintendo Entertainment System underwent a full redesign for the American release. Pretty slick, right?

| PART 2 |

VIDEO GAMES

Highlights from every Nintendo console.

VIDEO GAMES

While the basis of every game is "make it to the end," later games emphasize discovery and exploration, making the world feel thoroughly lived in.

MARIO EXPLAIN

Learn the basics of the main series.

| BY NOAH PETRILLO |

22   THE UNOFFICIAL GUIDE TO **MARIO**

The world of video games is a vastly diverse one. The type of game *Mario* is most renowned for, the type his creators mastered and made so popular, is called a "platform game," or "platformer."

Platformers are fairly straightforward. You play a character in a space filled with obstacles, and the goal is to move through the levels toward the end destination. In order to reach your destination, you must time your movements to land on objects (like platforms!) while avoiding hazards like spikes and enemies (like Goombas!). Along the way, you can acquire points for destroying enemies and earn power-ups that help you in some way. Within this framework, the possibilities are endless.

Many *Mario* adventures follow a similar plot: An evil leader invades a peaceful kingdom, captures their leader and scatters his minions throughout the land. Mario must venture across the kingdom through different landscapes, often into a castle, to defeat the evil mastermind and rescue a princess. However, certain games have made incredible departures from this basic outline. In *Super Mario Sunshine*, Mario is on a vacation with Princess Peach when he's falsely accused of littering all over the island resort. Being forced to clean the island with a special water-shooting device adds yet another unique layer to the platform style, as players wash away enemies and piles of muddy goop.

Whether it's rescuing an entire empire or trying to clean up his reputation, Mario has made a name for himself as the undisputed champion of platform games. He's far more than that, though—from RPGs to racing, arcade fighting, game shows and feature films, Mario is one of the most influential characters out there. As *IGN* writer Fran Mirabella puts it, Mario is to video games "what Mickey Mouse is to cartoons."

> "The series continues to capture our imagination and delight us in equal measure."
> **GAMESRADAR+**

PRESS ZL/ZR TO CROUCH

PRESS X/Y TO DASH

PRESS A/B TO JUMP

LEFT ANALOG STICK CONTROLS MARIO'S MOVEMENT

RIGHT ANALOG STICK CONTROLS THE CAMERA

In more modern games like *Super Mario Odyssey*, the "Joy-Cons" have motion controls—e.g., flicking your right wrist forward makes Mario throw his hat forward.

23

VIDEO GAMES

THE NINTENDO ENTERTAINMENT SYSTEM

This is the NES trilogy that started a video game revolution.

BY KYLE SCHMIDLIN

Released between 1985 and 1989 in North America, the original *Super Mario Bros.* trilogy for the Nintendo Entertainment System ignited a gaming revolution and established one of the world's most popular and recognizable mascots. More than 30 years later, the core character and gameplay elements introduced in these games still excite fans and inspire game designers. Every one of these games has been remastered or rereleased multiple times over numerous console generations, including on the Nintendo Switch. Mario and his supporting cast became the icons they are today by starring in these exceedingly polished, infinitely replayable classics.

The original NES has been displayed in art museums exhibiting the high points of gaming.

In 2021, the collectibles site *Rally* reported that an anonymous buyer purchased an unopened copy of *Super Mario Bros.* for $2 million. It's the most expensive game ever sold.

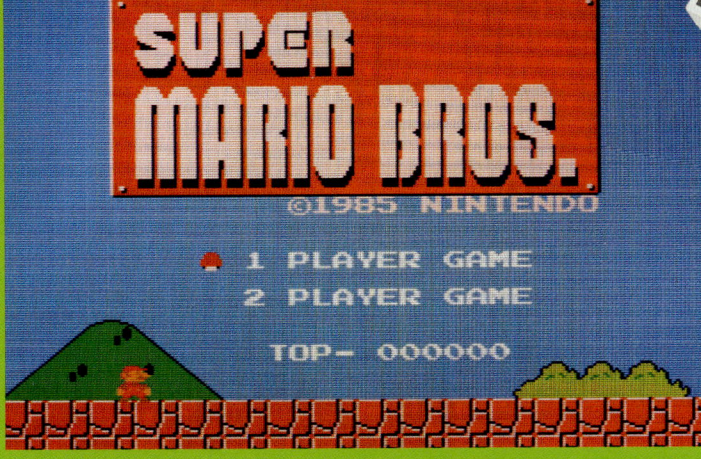

SUPER MARIO BROS.

EVERYONE GETS A COPY!

The original *Super Mario Bros.* was often sold with *Duck Hunt* on the same cartridge. In some cases, it was sold with a third game: *World Class Track Meet*. It was also packaged with the NES itself, so that most everyone who bought an NES ended up with a copy.

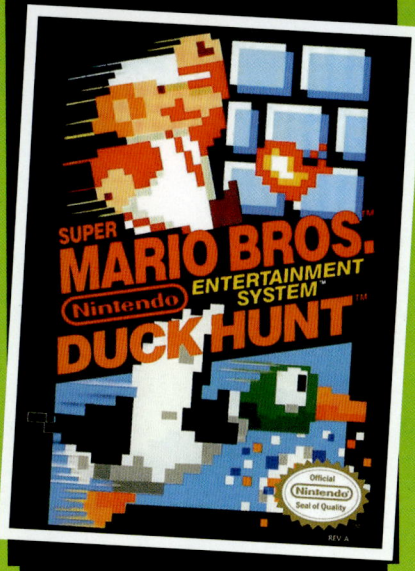

Originally released in 1985, *Super Mario Bros.* was unique and advanced compared to other games of the time. Its graphics were vibrant and detailed: Mario ran over green platforms, swam in blue water and jumped his way through gray castles. He faced a variety of enemies, each with distinct designs and attack patterns. He interacted in unique ways with blocks, springboards, warp pipes and climbable vines. The game blew the competition out of the water.

Designers Shigeru Miyamoto and Takashi Tezuka originally worked out the level layouts on graph paper. They designed the famous first level, 1-1, last, as a way to ease players into the game. Level 1-1 is deliberately forgiving, guiding the player to perform certain actions like jumping over Goombas and collecting super mushrooms.

That simple design philosophy of responsive, fun controls has carried on throughout the series and helped *Mario* stand above all the competition for nearly 40 years—and it would continue to be refined in every sequel since.

VIDEO GAMES

SUPER MARIO BROS. 2

In 1988, Nintendo had no established formula for sequels. *Super Mario Bros. 2* is a fairly significant departure from the first game, and the differences are obvious immediately. This time, four heroes are playable: Mario, Luigi, Princess Toadstool and Toad. When Level 1-1 begins, before you can even move, you're free-falling down a seemingly bottomless pit. This time, Mario and his friends don't just move left to right—they also climb into the clouds and dig their way into ruins.

Anything goes in the Mushroom Kingdom, but Subcon, the world of *Super Mario Bros. 2*, is somehow even weirder. Instead of pipes, Mario and his friends tunnel into vases. Whenever Mario grabs a key, a creepy mask called Phanto chases him until he finds the door it unlocks. Sometimes, instead of pulling a turnip out of the ground, Mario will pull out a potion that lets him create a door to a shadowy subworld. There are flying magic carpets and three-headed snakes, and some levels are completed by crawling into an eagle's beak.

One explanation for all the changes and oddities comes at the end of the game, when it turns out to have all been part of Mario's dream. But the real reason is that this wasn't originally a *Mario* game at all. In Japan, the game was released as *Yume Kōjō: Doki Doki Panic*. Still, it had *Mario* elements in its DNA. The game's director, Kensuke Tanabe, recalls that when the game was still in a prototype state, Miyamoto told him to "make something a little more *Mario*-like," adding, "As long as it's fun, anything goes."

SUPER MARIO BROS. 3

With the final chapter in the mainline NES trilogy, Mario moved back, closer to his roots—and yet reached far greater heights than he ever had. *Super Mario Bros. 3* is the inspired culmination of all the ideas Miyamoto and his team had implemented to this point, and it's widely regarded as one of the best *Mario* games ever.

While the gameplay is more in line with the first game, it's clear that Miyamoto's team pushed themselves to a creative high point. There are more power-ups in this game than in almost any other *Mario* game before or since. The level design is more creative and varied than ever, with horizontal and vertical challenges, pipe mazes, stage hazards like tornadoes and an Angry Sun and alternate paths in almost every level. There's a world where all the enemies are gigantic and another with a fortress that stretches into the clouds. It's a marvel of interactive art.

DRESSED FOR ANY OCCASION

Mario can strap on the furry Tanooki suit, which lets him fly around and turn into an invincible statue; wear the Frog suit, which makes swimming a breeze; or armor up with the Hammer Bros. suit, which gives him a protective helmet and lets him throw hammers back at the Koopas. In an interview translated by *Nintendo Everything*, Takashi Tezuka said, "We crammed all sorts of things for people to find into every single stage, so you could replay the same one over and over and still find new ways to do things." And it's true.

FROG MARIO

VIDEO GAMES

THE SUPER NINTENDO ENTERTAINMENT SYSTEM (SNES)

New hardware allows Mario to branch out like never before.

BY KYLE SCHMIDLIN

As Nintendo's breakout mascot, Mario had become synonymous with video game quality. With a new console generation on the horizon, the world was curious how Nintendo would evolve the franchise. The answer was to make one final, traditional 2D *Mario* masterpiece and then put the plumber in charge of conquering new frontiers in various spinoffs, racing games and more as-yet uncharted terrain.

28 THE UNOFFICIAL GUIDE TO **MARIO**

SUPER MARIO WORLD

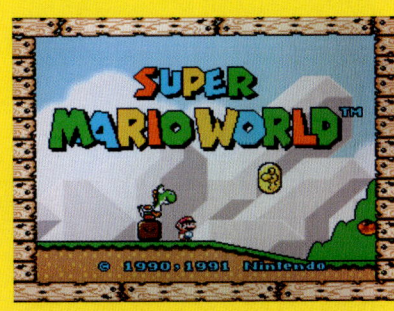

YOSHI

Early in the development of *Super Mario World*, the game was known as *Super Mario Bros. 4*, and looked an awful lot like the third game. But the developers really wanted to set the game apart and show off what their new hardware could do. By the time the Super Nintendo was ready to release, the game took on a more unique identity and arguably became the crown jewel of 2D *Mario* games.

Once inside a level, players are greeted with colorful new enemies, redesigns of old enemies and new level designs. Most levels contain alternate paths, and many levels contain secret exits that Mario must find to truly complete the game.

Mario's new, more robust moveset is implemented beautifully thanks to the most fluid and responsive controls yet. The new Cape Feather power-up gives Mario a cape that he can use to take out enemies and fly through the air. As long as there's nothing in the way, Mario can skip entire levels by flying over them.

But the game's greatest innovation and most lasting contribution is the introduction of Yoshi, Mario's rideable dinosaur companion. Yoshi can retrieve items stashed behind unbreakable walls, walk across dangerous terrain and, in some variations, grow wings and fly. Mario can even clear larger gaps by taking a second jump off Yoshi's back, sending him down to the pit below.

29

VIDEO GAMES

SUPER MARIO WORLD 2: YOSHI'S ISLAND

Released in 1995, *Yoshi's Island* is one of the most graphically impressive games on the SNES. The game's distinct, coloring book look was achieved by digitally scanning hand-drawn images and then recreating them painstakingly, pixel by pixel.

Apart from the game's look, the most immediate difference is that Yoshi is now the star. The game takes place in the past, when Mario, Luigi and Bowser were babies. Baby Luigi is a prisoner of the evil wizard Kamek, and Baby Mario rides on the backs of Yoshis through Yoshi's Island to rescue his brother.

Levels in *Yoshi's Island* are far more open and expansive than ever before. Each level has three kinds of collectibles, and unlocking everything in the game requires collecting them all. The branching paths, hidden items and different options for traversal make the levels of *Yoshi's Island* the densest in any *Mario* game yet.

For its colorful graphics, catchy music and memorable boss battles, the often-overlooked *Yoshi's Island* has gone on to become a classic.

Many Yoshis came together to ensure the safe reuniting of Baby Mario and Baby Luigi.

30   THE UNOFFICIAL GUIDE TO **MARIO**

MORE MARIO CLASSICS

The success of this rerelease showed the longevity of *Mario* games.

You can play three full games on this cartridge!

The *Super Mario RPG: Legend of the Seven Stars* title screen.

Other *Mario* titles for the SNES would see gaming's most iconic superstar venture into totally new genres. The most consequential of these, **Super Mario Kart**, was originally released in 1992. This humble game became a big hit, but it was only the first in a long-running series that would become one of Nintendo's most financially lucrative.

Super Mario All-Stars, released in 1993, collected Mario's first three NES adventures on a single cartridge, updating their graphics and adding save states. It also introduced American gamers to *The Lost Levels*, the previously Japan-only sequel to the original *Super Mario Bros.*

Later, Nintendo partnered with Square, the producers of the *Final Fantasy* series of games, to create a role-playing game starring Mario. **Super Mario RPG: Legend of the Seven Stars** released in 1996, and the platforming star took to the RPG setting like a natural. Vibrant characters and worlds, fun dialogue and an intuitive battle system made it one of the most accessible RPGs on the console.

MARIO'S RPG CREW

VIDEO GAMES

MARIO KART

The fun revs up with a racing theme.

BY NOAH PETRILLO

The number of racers was exciting from the first iteration—and it's only grown since.

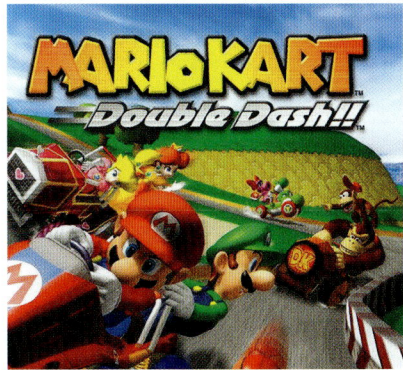

When Mario and all his friends and foes aren't vying to either save or take over the Mushroom Kingdom and beyond, they're often taking part in activities together. Perhaps the single most popular pastime of the *Mario* universe is go-kart racing, and it has caught on with gamers all over the world.

In 1992, *Super Mario Kart* was released, featuring a cast of classic characters including Mario himself, Luigi, Princess Peach, Yoshi, Toad, Bowser, Koopa Troopa and Donkey Kong Jr. The first *Mario* racing game included not just tracks in recognizable locations but also various items with different effects that could be used to hinder the progress of fellow racers. Green shells shoot straight and bounce, red shells home in on you like a missile, bananas cause you to spin out, mushrooms allow you to boost and stars give you temporary invincibility and increased speed. It also introduced difficulty levels as 50cc, 100cc and 150cc, both increasing in the speed of the karts as well as the skill of the AI racers.

The first *Mario Kart* offered different racing styles based on the character you pick. For example, Mario and Luigi are fairly balanced racers. Heavier racers like Bowser can reach a higher speed but have low acceleration. The opposite is true of Toad, who can accelerate fast but has a lower top speed.

Mario and Luigi showcase their epic and lightning-fast partnership in *Double Dash!!*.

The next iteration, *Mario Kart 64*, saw the increase of possible players from two to four, as well as improvements in graphics due to the higher processing power of the Nintendo 64. With better graphics, the racetracks were able to rise and lower in elevation and introduce pits and other obstacles.

DIAL UP THE ACTION!

Released in 2019, *Mario Kart Tour* is designed to play on your smartphone. You can play online with friends in weekly tournaments that offer three races plus a bonus challenge. The mobile game features unique races from major cities all over the world, including New York, Tokyo, London and more!

VIDEO GAMES

Fan-Favorite Courses From All Over Mushroom Kingdom

Mario Circuit 1 (SNES) The very first racetrack in the series, the remaster of this iconic track proves it still holds up as a fun race that infuses a ton of nostalgia.

Maple Treeway (Wii) This track features gorgeous autumn views along with piles of leaves as obstacles.

Baby Park (GameCube) It's just a small circle track with more laps than the usual three, yet the tension on this track is unparalleled as you're hit with way more objects.

Rainbow Road (Switch) Every game gets a Rainbow Road, and they're all great, but the latest edition boasts new jumps and a track destined for an outer space location.

One of the most beloved installments in the *Mario Kart* series debuted on the GameCube in 2003 and was built around the idea of playing with friends. *Mario Kart Double Dash!!* saw another round of great new features, like different go-karts that exemplify each character. Additionally, there were new characters you could unlock by winning races. By winning the "Special Cup" at 100cc, you unlock Toad and Toadette as well as their go-kart.

Unlike any *Mario Kart* games before or after, you race in pairs, where one character races and the other fires objects. Part of the fun is being able to switch who is driving and who is throwing

34 THE UNOFFICIAL GUIDE TO MARIO

objects throughout the race.

With the release of *Mario Kart Wii* came the advent of a wheel-shaped controller. Thanks to the motion controls of the Nintendo Wii, you can twist and turn the wheel like you would in a real go-kart, adding an extra sense of realism and immersion to the fun.

The storied and beloved history of these games culminated in the 2017 release of *Mario Kart 8 Deluxe*, which was a reissue of the Wii U's *Mario Kart 8*. IGN remarked, "It's just as amazing in 2017 as it was in 2014." And today, it's still amazing.

Classic characters have different outfit options, like Cat Peach and Tanooki Mario.

"65% of players said they wouldn't let their partner win at *Mario Kart*."
—PCMAG

Mario Kart 8 Deluxe is widely considered the culmination of every previous *Mario Kart*.

VIDEO GAMES

THE NINTENDO 64 & SUPER MARIO 64

Jumpman jumps to the third dimension.

BY JOSEPH RAUCH

When the Nintendo 64, or N64—the company's first product that would fully step from 2D to 3D gaming—finally made its North American debut in September 1996, only two titles were available. Nintendo's fiercest competitor, Sony, had launched its PlayStation with eight accompanying titles, and the hardware had been available in the U.S. since September 1995. One of Nintendo's two launch titles was *Pilotwings*, a 3D flight simulator that did not feature any of Nintendo's iconic characters. The other game: *Super Mario 64*. Nintendo gambled the fate of its home console—and by extension their entire business—on whether "Jumpman" could jump spectacularly into the third dimension.

36 THE UNOFFICIAL GUIDE TO MARIO

The Nintendo 64 is often considered the company's coolest-looking console.

VIDEO GAMES

Mario strikes a pose whenever he finds a hidden star, often flashing a peace sign at the camera.

Consumers around the world purchased more than 11 million copies of *Mario 64*, and the N64 immediately sold out in the U.S.

In a retrospective about his time working at Babbage's (now GameStop) during the launch of the N64, *Ars Technica* contributor Lee Hutchinson wrote, "The rule that a console must have a broad spectrum of launch titles to appeal to the North American audience was generally true, but Nintendo found the exception: a single amazing title, with well-implemented 3D gameplay that most console players had never experienced, could bear the weight of the entire system on its shoulders."

Unfortunately for Nintendo, *Mario 64* did not carry the console to victory in the console wars of the '90s as the PlayStation 1 sold three times as many units as the N64. The greater value of the Nintendo 64 is its legacy. *Mario 64* pioneered the video game genre of 3D platformers, games that focused on running and jumping around in 3D spaces via the analog stick. Before *Mario 64*, most gamers simply had to settle for D-pad controls (four separate buttons for each cardinal direction) that offered limited movement. The launch title introduced new moves that would become staples in future 3D *Mario* games. The already athletic plumber could now triple jump, ground pound, long jump, dive and somersault.

Princess Peach's Castle in *Mario 64* popularized the game design mechanic of a "hub world" that connected the player to all other levels. Without that castle, we most likely wouldn't have gamer-favorite hub worlds such as Gruntilda's Lair, Delfino Plaza, Comet Observatory or Garreg Mach Monastery.

38 THE UNOFFICIAL GUIDE TO MARIO

Not including *Mario 64*, two titles in the N64 library mark milestones in video game history and regularly appear on lists of greatest video games of all time. They are:

- **GoldenEye 007** Seen as "the blueprint for console first-person shooters." —Alex Simmons, *IGN*
- **The Legend of Zelda: Ocarina of Time** First 3D *Zelda* game, highest-rated game ever on Metacritic.

The N64 kicked off other franchises that are still running today and have raked in billions for Nintendo. Here's their breakdown by year:

- **1998: Mario Party** 25 installments across several types of hardware.
- **1999: Super Smash Bros.** Often referred to as *Smash 64*, this game launched another successful franchise for Nintendo. With five games and counting, it's the fifth biggest bestseller of all time.
- **2000: Paper Mario** There are now six games in this series.

No matter how many years go by in the 3D era, we will always be able to trace roots back to the Nintendo 64 and *Super Mario 64*.

VIDEO GAMES

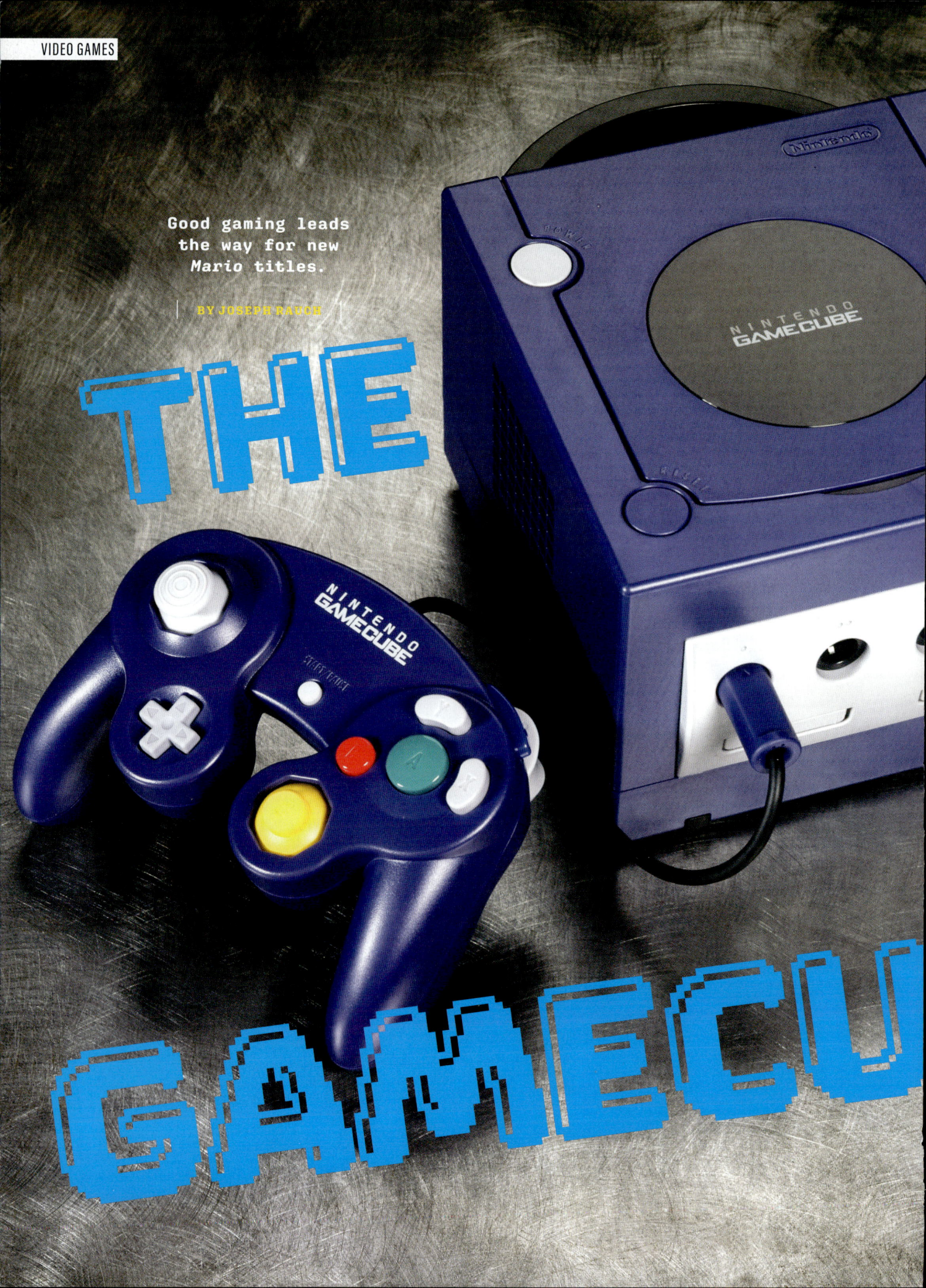

Good gaming leads the way for new *Mario* titles.

BY JOSEPH RAUCH

THE GAMECU

Mario finally gets a moment of rest on what was supposed to be a relaxing vacation in *Super Mario Sunshine*.

Compared to the N64 era, 2001 was not a time for innovation in home consoles. 3D had become the norm, so there were no more dimensions to leap into. The analog stick had become standard, and motion controls were a distant dream.

To cut costs and compete in the home console market, Nintendo temporarily abandoned cartridges and joined Sony and Microsoft in creating discs for their new millennium home console, the GameCube. Unlike the PlayStation 2 and Xbox, however, the GameCube could not play DVDs due to its smaller disc drive. This would ultimately be one of the reasons Sony and Microsoft crushed Nintendo during the console wars of the early 2000s.

The GameCube's North American launch in November 2001 did not boast any titles from franchises such as *Mario*, *Donkey Kong* or *Super Smash Bros*. But in July 2002, Nintendo had a chance to wow latecomers with *Super Mario Sunshine*, a game that sees Mario take a vacation to Isle Delfino, a tropical paradise, only to be framed for pollution.

VIDEO GAMES

The GameCube saw releases from other major franchises like *Jimmy Neutron*, *Batman* and Pixar's *The Incredibles*.

Super Mario Sunshine was Nintendo's first foray into scripted voice acting with full lines of dialogue. One big change, for example, is that instead of only grunting and laughing, Bowser and Bowser Jr. actually conversed with each other. Unfortunately, the average Nintendo fan thought the voice acting was terrible. Perhaps it's not a coincidence that Nintendo didn't revisit this type of voice acting until *The Super Mario Bros. Movie* (see pg. 62).

In 2021, *Nintendo Everything* interviewed Scott Burns about his experience voicing the *Super Mario Sunshine* iteration of Bowser. When asked for his thoughts on gamers' negative reaction, Burns said, "I think some fans probably would have liked to have the voice be more fierce, and I'd have to agree with them. If I could do him now, I'd like to put a bit more nuance into the performance as well." Maybe Jack Black, the voice actor for the 2023 film version of Bowser, read that article or watched the Bowser cutscenes in *Sunshine* as his fierce take on the character has been well-received.

Fortunately for Nintendo, the GameCube had plenty of *Mario* titles that were beloved and relatively free from debate. Most critics and fans still consider the GameCube's iteration of *Paper Mario* to be the highest quality in the series.

"Offering a great plot, fun traveling companions, witty dialogue, and a fun battle system, *Paper Mario: The Thousand-Year Door*, seriously, is not only the best *Paper Mario* game but also one of the best RPGs of all time," wrote *iMore* Gaming Editor Rebecca Spear.

In addition to continuing successful series from the N64, the GameCube offered the first *Mario*-themed soccer game, *Super Mario Strikers*. There are now three entries in the series.

Super Smash Bros. Melee is the only past-generation game in the *Smash Bros.* series that maintains a vibrant competitive scene. The game endeared many generations of gamers to the GameCube controller, often touted as the best gaming controller ever made. Even while playing *Super Smash Bros. Ultimate*, the latest game in the series, most professional players opt for GameCube controller replicas over modern controllers.

The GameCube's console hardware may have been behind the times, but its controller and beloved library of games have proven to be timeless. ■

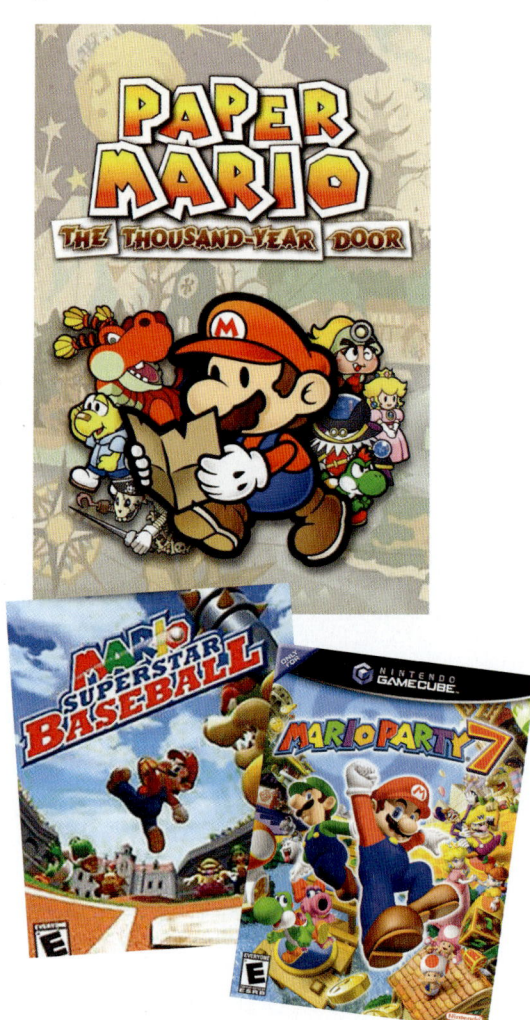

The Gamecube also saw Mario's venture into baseball as well as the seventh installment of the *Mario Party* series.

42 THE UNOFFICIAL GUIDE TO MARIO

Best of the GameCube *Mario* Games

To make sure you don't miss any hits, we're going to be flexible about what we consider a *Mario* game. We're counting all titles that include Mario or branch out from his universe.

Mario Kart: Double Dash!!

Of the 14 *Mario Kart* games in the franchise so far, critics and fans usually place *Double Dash!!* somewhere in the top three. This was the first and only game in the series where two characters could ride on one kart and switch positions, allowing for different special-item capabilities.

"The same awe that many felt seeing tracks realized in 3D is amplified so much."
—RabbidLuigi,
popular video game YouTuber

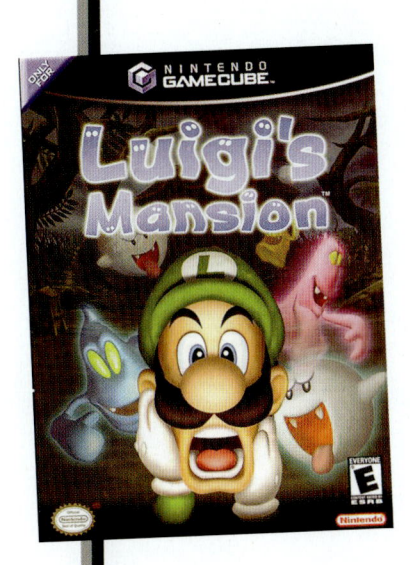

Luigi's Mansion

Luigi finally got his name in the title of a game! When Mario goes missing, it's up to Luigi to explore a haunted mansion and battle ghosts using a *Mario* universe–style version of a ghostbusting vacuum.

"Its mechanics and gameplay, while simple, are still quite enjoyable to play and the graphics hold up very nicely for a launch title in 2001."
—Game Rant

Mario Party 5

Because the *Mario Party* series has a long history with many installments, there have been ups and downs. *Mario Party 5* was definitely an up. The game boasted sharper graphics and continued beloved mechanics from previous entries.

"As a multiplayer party game, *Mario Party 5* is a must-have."
—IGN

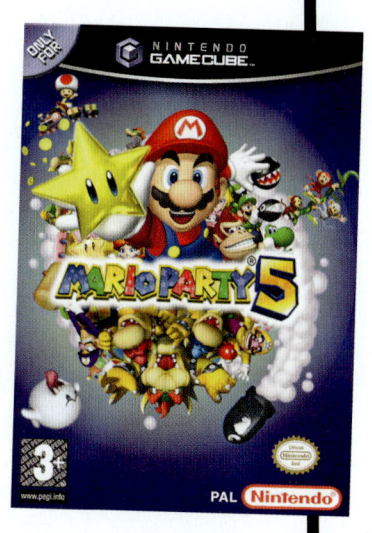

VIDEO GAMES

SUPER SMASH BROS.

Mario throws down with other Nintendo characters.

BY JOSEPH RAUCH

Which video game characters can Mario beat in a fight? The Nintendo 64's *Super Smash Bros.* was the first answer to this question. In 1996, Kirby co-creators Satoru Iwata and Masahiro Sakurai started developing a platform fighting game that would become *Super Smash Bros.* Iwata, who would be Nintendo's president and CEO from 2002 until his passing in 2015, said of *Smash 64*, "I felt something special about this title from the very first moment I started programming for it." The game went on to be a smash hit, presenting core gameplay mechanics that have now endured for nearly three decades:

■ 2D fighting on "stages" and platforms (first *Mario* stages were Peach's Castle, Mushroom Kingdom and Super Happy Tree)
■ Defeating an opponent by knocking them into the "blast zone," which is mostly off screen
■ Building up damage by attacking, and higher damage making it easier to knock someone into the blast zone
■ The option of using items that appear randomly
■ Being able to grab the ledge on either side of a stage ■

44 THE UNOFFICIAL GUIDE TO **MARIO**

BRAWL

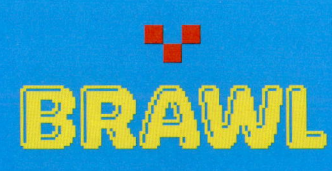

Year Released 2008
System Wii
New Mario Universe Playable Character Wario
New Mario Universe Stages Delfino Plaza, Mushroomy Kingdom, Mario Circuit, Yoshi's Island
Notable New Game Mechanics
- Random tripping (very unpopular; removed afterward)
- Final smash moves that are specific to characters and can only be used via items
- Building your own stages

"For the first time, the list of guests includes third-party, non-Nintendo characters such as Solid Snake and Sonic the Hedgehog, and all of them bring their own signature fighting styles and moves to the game."
—*GameSpot*

MELEE

Year Released 2001
System GameCube
New Mario Universe Playable Characters Peach, Bowser, Dr. Mario
New Mario Universe Stages Rainbow Cruise, Princess Peach's Castle, Yoshi's Story
Notable New Game Mechanics
- Spot dodging (pressing down and shield at the same time allows you to be intangible for a moment but leaves you vulnerable after; useful for avoiding grabs and stun on your shield)
- Air dodging (allows you to become momentarily intangible while in the air)
- Side-B special move (before, there was only B, up B, down B)
- Unofficial advanced techniques (not in the tutorial) such as wavedashing, wavelanding and dash dancing
- Teching on walls and wall jumping
- More taunt options

Battle your friends with your favorite character, using objects like Poké Balls (above). It may mean the difference between victory and defeat.

"Originally thought to be a minor upgrade to the original, *SSB Melee* returns chock full of so many options and features it will make you dizzy." —*IGN*

VIDEO GAMES

SUPER SMASH BROS.
FOR NINTENDO 3DS AND WII U

(often called *Smash 4* for short)

Year Released 2014

New Mario Universe Playable Characters Rosalina and Luma, Bowser Jr.

New Mario Universe Stages 3D Land, Golden Plains, Rainbow Road, Paper Mario, Super Mario Maker

Notable New Game Mechanics
- Characters you can purchase and download
- Custom moves
- Customizable Mii characters

"In many ways, *Super Smash Bros.* for Wii U feels like a direct response to criticisms of its party-friendly aspirations."
—*Nintendo Life*

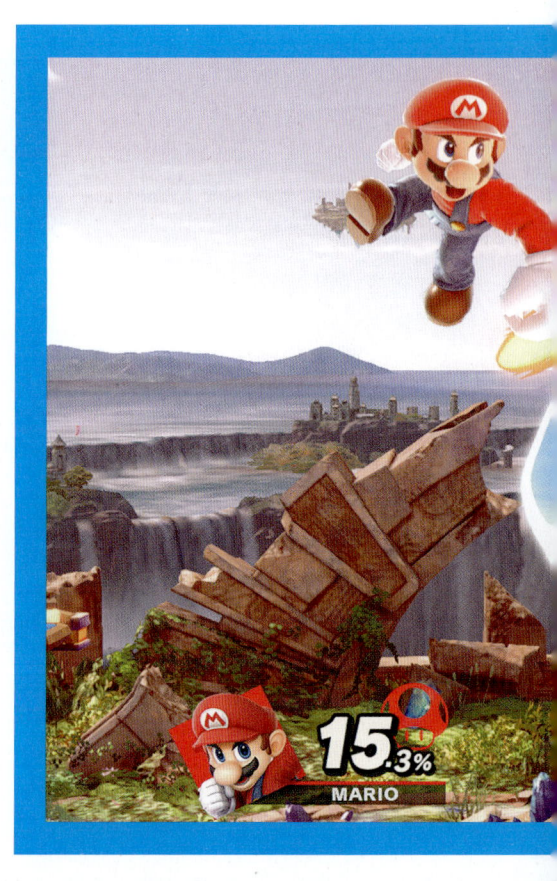

Take Control of the Fight!

Never used a Gamecube controller? Here are the basic buttons and what they do. Once you get these down, you'll find that combinations will serve you well.

Z Button
Shield to block hits and "tech" (recover quickly from a big hit by pressing as you hit the ground)

Main Analog Stick
Walk/run left and right; push down to crouch, push up to jump

D-Pad
Taunt (strike a pose to disrespect your opponent; some taunts do damage)

SUPER SMASH BROS. ULTIMATE

Year Released 2018
New Mario Universe Playable Characters Daisy, Piranha Plant
New Mario Universe Stage New Donk City Hall
"This is the ultimate *Smash Bros.* because its scope is so massive that it's hard to imagine adding anything else." —*Polygon*

Y Button
Press this to jump

L/R Button
Grab opponents to hold them steady while you hit them

X Button
Also used as a jump button

A Button
A only = jab;
Slightly holding a direction, then immediately pressing A = tilt attack;
Hitting A and a direction at the same time = smash attack

B Button
A different type of special attack, depending on whether you press B with no analog stick movement or hold the analog stick up or down (later, side B would become an option)

C Stick
Push this in any direction to unleash a heavy attack

VIDEO GAMES

ON THE WII

New technology breathes new life into our favorite plumber.

| BY NOAH PETRILLO |

Super Mario Bros. Wii gave players the classic 2D platform experience with updated graphics and even more new features.

48 THE UNOFFICIAL GUIDE TO **MARIO**

The Nintendo Wii sent shockwaves through the world of video games with its release in 2006. With a comparatively low price and revolutionary motion controls, the new Nintendo system shot to the top spot of the console wars, outselling the Xbox 360 and PlayStation 3 in the first years of their releases. The major defining feature of the Wii is its controller, the Wii Remote. Unlike most other controllers, it's shaped more like a television remote and relies equally on button pushing and arm and wrist motions. It has an attachable second piece called the "Nunchuk" that includes an analog stick and extra buttons for more elaborate games. *Mario* fit snugly into this new era of gaming, returning with new versions of familiar installments and bold strides into new territory.

Twenty-one years after the game's initial release in Japan, American gamers finally got to experience the original sequel to *Super Mario Bros.* The game was released as part of a package called *Super Mario All-Stars*, celebrating *Mario*'s 25th anniversary. While the games themselves were merely a direct port from their original forms on the NES and SNES, *Mario* fans joyously attempted to clear the exceedingly difficult levels that Nintendo decided were too hardcore for American gamers in the late 1980s.

In keeping with the legendary status of the original *Super Mario Bros.* trilogy, one of the more surprising hits from the Wii era was *New Super Mario Bros. Wii*, a 2D platformer released in 2009. Receiving an 8.9/10 from *IGN*'s official review, the game was particularly popular with families, as this was the first time anyone could play a *Mario* platformer with up to four players.

"A game that keeps a smile on a player's face is a wonderful thing."
SHIGERU MIYAMOTO

The galaxy is yours to explore in this addicting and undeniably beautiful gaming experience.

49

VIDEO GAMES

The motion controls of the Wii also came in handy for the many *Mario* sports games that were released on the console. With *Mario Power Tennis*, for example, you played the game much like you would real tennis, by swinging your arm at the right time to hit the ball over the net. It was an incredibly seamless playing style that felt unbelievably satisfying. Similarly, *Mario Super Sluggers* "makes great use of the Wii Remote," according to *Game Rant*.

Perhaps the greatest *Mario* games to appear on the Wii are a rare example of Nintendo sticking with the same formula and everyone being happier for it. The first *Super Mario Galaxy* is regarded by many to be one of the greatest platformer games of all time. *IGN* rated the game 9.7/10, calling it "the spiritual sequel to *Super Mario 64*." The story starts rather similarly to the others, but this time, Bowser rips Princess Peach's castle from its very foundations and whisks it away into outer space! The visuals in the opening sequence are the most stunning to date. Mario then makes his way to a spaceship that acts as the hub world, where Rosalina, the keeper of the ship, shows you doorways that take you to different galaxies in search of Peach and her castle.

The 2010 sequel, *Super Mario Galaxy 2*, is rated even higher, receiving 10/10 ratings by both *GameSpot* and *IGN*. While the backdrop is largely the same, the game includes intuitive little features for new players. For example, if you keep dying in a section, Rosalina will appear and offer you tips. It's clear the developers at Nintendo poured their hearts and souls into refining the playing experience for as wide an audience as possible. The result is nothing short of perfection.

Fans were delighted at the inclusion of Yoshi in *Super Mario Galaxy 2*.

While Mario and Luigi have a habit of defeating Wario and Waluigi, the evil friends have a chance to settle the score with a tennis match!

Using the motion controls, playing *Super Sluggers* feels as close to the real thing as games can get.

VIDEO GAMES

MARIO SPORTS

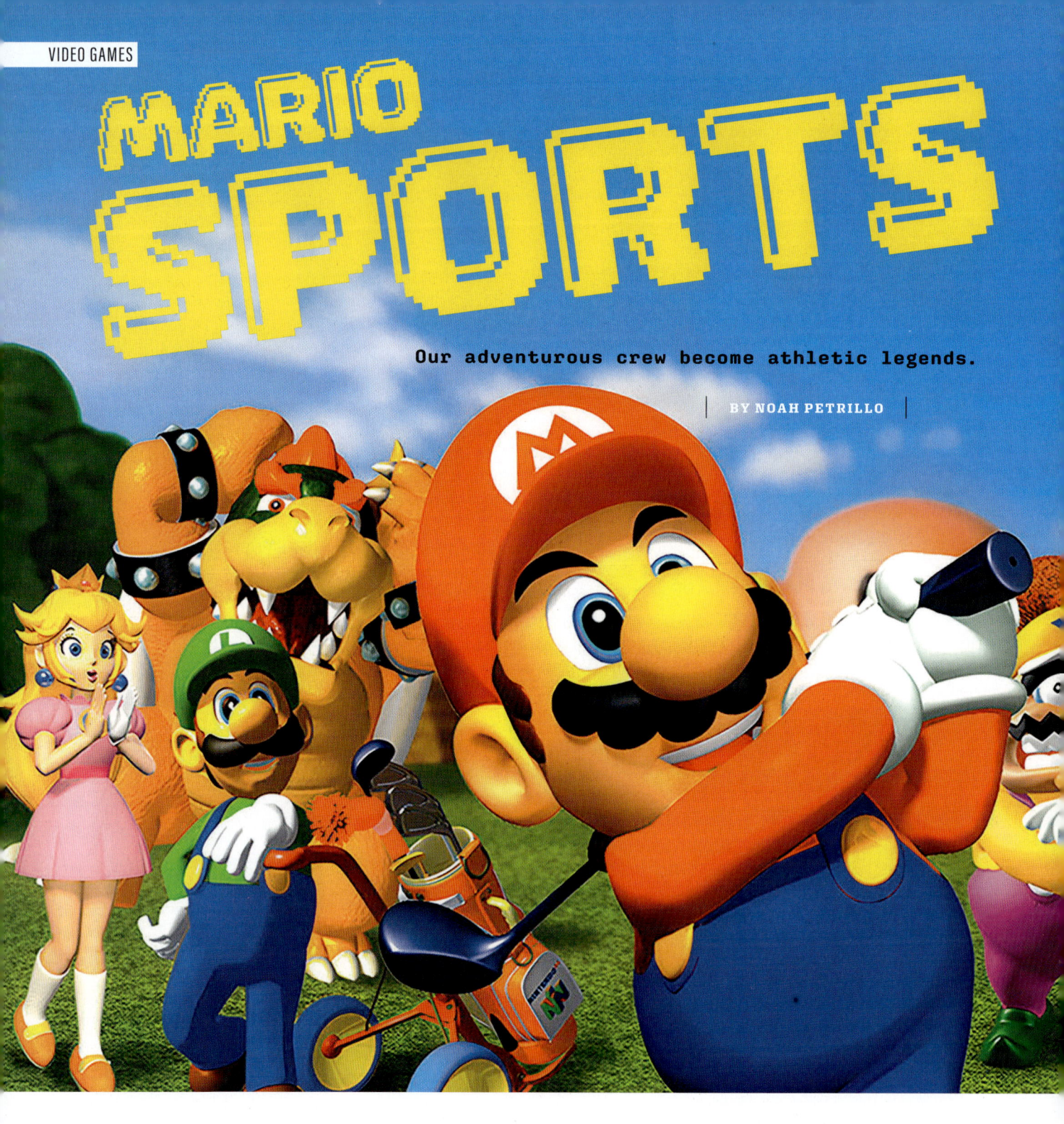

Our adventurous crew become athletic legends.

| BY NOAH PETRILLO |

It may come as a surprise, but Mario and his pals have dipped their toes into nearly every major sport in existence. With almost too many to mention, here's a highlight reel of the best.

Mario & Sonic at the Olympic Winter Games (Wii)
When *Mario & Sonic at the Olympic Winter Games* was released in 2009, the formula was fresh and the games were super chill and tons of fun. Some of the best experiences of this kinetic crossover are its minigames, like Ice Hockey and Downhill Skiing.

Mario Golf (N64)
The first major sports game to feature Mario, this remains a classic among fans and critics alike. While essentially a straightforward golf game with *Mario* skins, this no-nonsense experience hit the right players at the right time.

Mario Strikers Charged (Wii)
The sequel to *Super Mario Strikers*, *Mario Strikers Charged* is a systematic improvement on its predecessor. With better graphics and more satisfying and frequent

52 THE UNOFFICIAL GUIDE TO MARIO

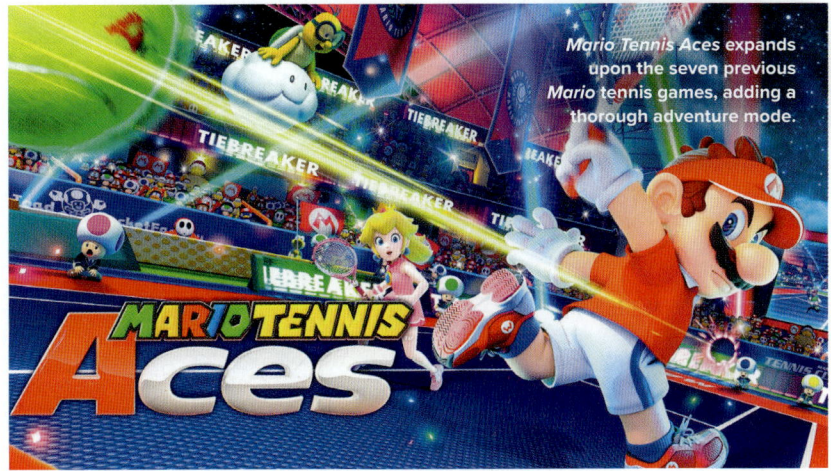

From the NES to the Switch, *Mario* sports games have always been part of the franchise.

Characters in this fan-favorite *Mario* sports game are outfitted with mechalike suits to increase their speed and kicking power.

The Wii remote has played a major role in sports games both inside and outside of the *Mario* universe.

Mario Tennis Aces expands upon the seven previous *Mario* tennis games, adding a thorough adventure mode.

skill shots, *Screen Rant* deems this installment "one of the most exhilarating multiplayer games in Nintendo's library."

Mario Tennis Aces (Switch)
If fluid motion controls are your thing, this title is definitely worth checking out. *GameSpew* muses that it's "one of the best Mario sports games we've ever played."

53

VIDEO GAMES

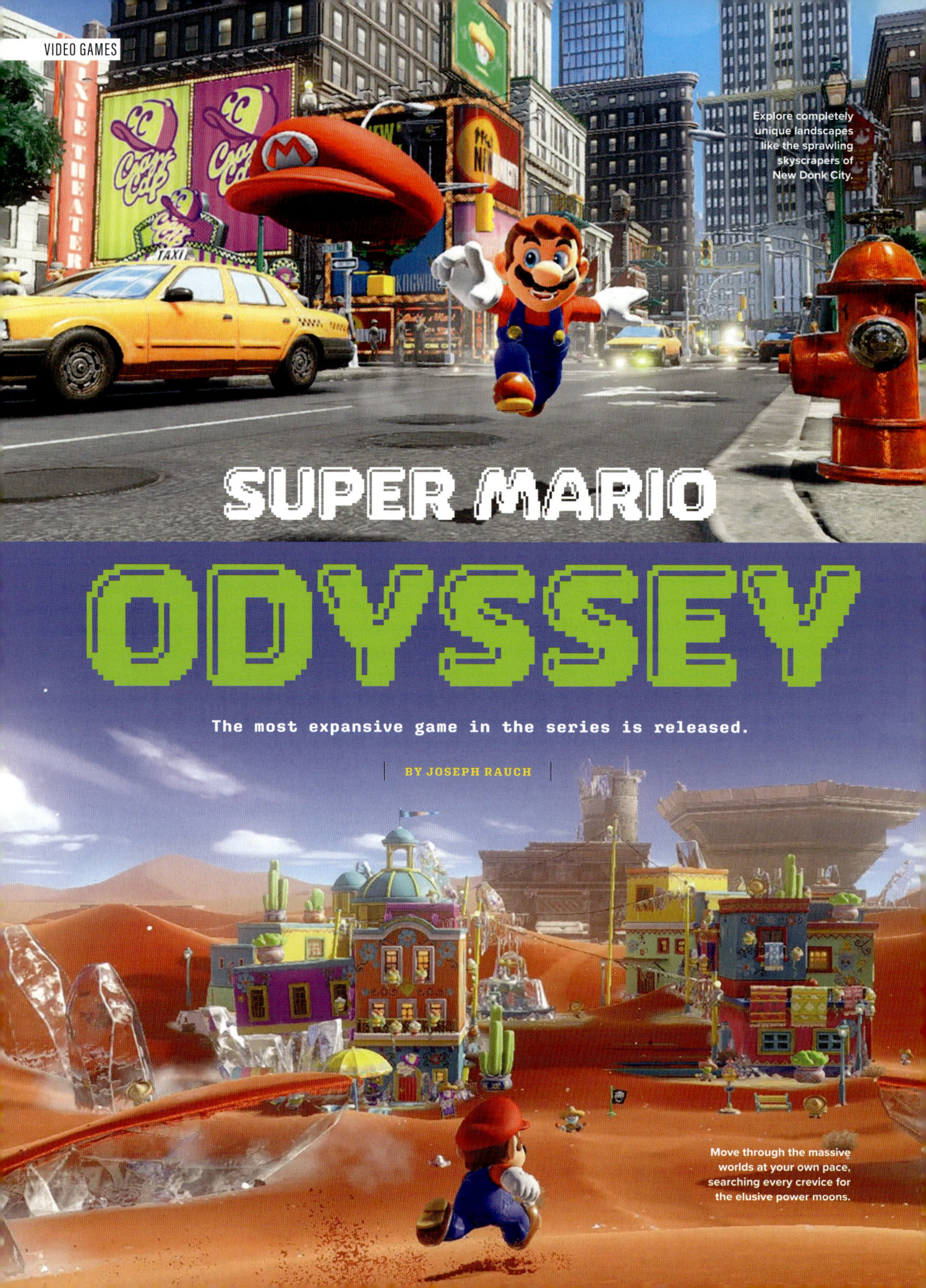

Explore completely unique landscapes like the sprawling skyscrapers of New Donk City.

SUPER MARIO ODYSSEY

The most expansive game in the series is released.

BY JOSEPH RAUCH

Move through the massive worlds at your own pace, searching every crevice for the elusive power moons.

The Switch provides the improved ability to play on your TV or take your games with you wherever you go!

When it comes to the Nintendo Switch's iteration of the 3D *Mario* game series, *Super Mario Odyssey*, there are two main qualities that differentiate the title from its predecessors:

1 **There's Cappy, a sentient hat who joins Mario on his quest to save Princess Peach for the umpteenth time.** By throwing, jumping and buttstomping on Cappy, Mario can increase his agility and offensive maneuvers. Perhaps most importantly, Cappy can possess many of the living creatures and objects in the world of *Odyssey*. This magic allows Mario to pilot these beings and use their special abilities.

2 **Of all the 3D *Mario* games, *Odyssey* has the most "open" world so far.** Most 3D *Mario* games to date involve entering a level and being limited to a single mission where players earn a star or shine sprite. After achieving the mission, the game usually teleports players back to the hub world or to the entrance of the level.

In *Odyssey*, you can stay in the level as long as you want and easily traverse the map. There are few restrictions on the order in which players find "moons," the *Odyssey* version of stars. Levels are bigger, and there are 880 moons to find.

Super Mario Odyssey won two 2018 BAFTA Games Awards for Game Design and Best Family Game, and so far, 27.65 million copies have been purchased. If you haven't already, consider getting in line to board the *Odyssey*. ■

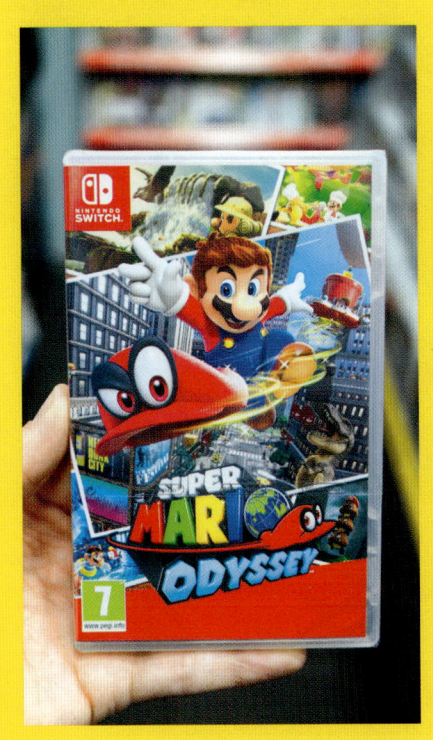

> "I literally applauded as the credits rolled on *Super Mario Odyssey*."
> —RYAN MCCAFFREY, *IGN*

SWITCH IT UP!

In addition to *Super Mario Odyssey*, there are a couple of other must-have *Mario* titles on the Switch.

■ **Super Mario Maker 2**
Create 2D *Mario* levels. Then play them, along with levels other people have created. "This sequel might be the most accessible game design tool ever created." —*IGN*

■ **Mario + Rabbids Kingdom Battle**
If you like *Fire Emblem* and *Mario* games, this title will be a special fusion for you. The Rabbids are a fun bonus.

55

VIDEO GAMES

TOP 10

Games on this list were considered based on their design, their fun factor and the size of their legacy and impact. If you really want to see what all the *Mario* fuss is about, check out these 10 games as soon as you can.

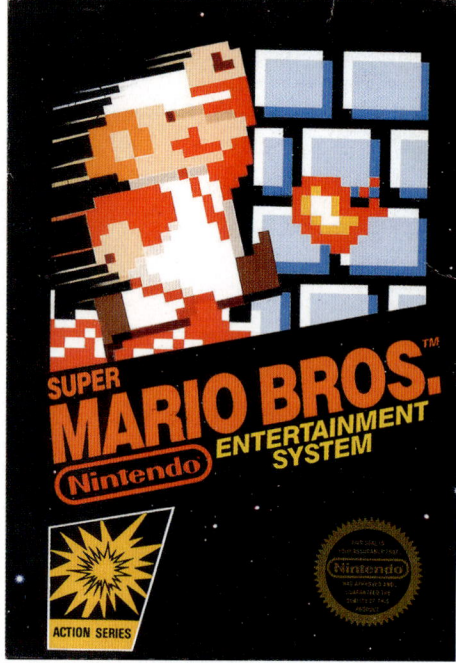

10 Super Mario Bros.
This revolutionary game still holds up. Beginners can walk through the levels, deal with every obstacle and fight every enemy. A pro can speed through each stage, jump over everything and use warps to get to the end quickly. The choice is yours, and this philosophy of freedom and fun would carry through virtually every *Mario* game.

9 Super Mario Maker 2
The world has come a long way since Shigeru Miyamoto and Takashi Tezuka first mapped out *Mario* levels on graph paper. Now, anyone can create their own levels with the intuitive level creator of *Super Mario Maker 2* and share their innovative creations with gamers all over the world.

8 Super Mario RPG: Legend of the Seven Stars
Mario's first role-playing adventure takes a more accessible approach to the genre. *Legend of the Seven Stars* features exotic locales and some of the quirkiest characters ever seen in a video game, and it's all set to one of our favorite, most robust soundtracks in the franchise.

56 THE UNOFFICIAL GUIDE TO **MARIO**

TITLES

These are Mario's best of all time!

BY KYLE SCHMIDLIN

7 Paper Mario: The Thousand-Year Door
Within the *Paper Mario* franchise of RPGs, *The Thousand-Year Door* is the undeniable standout. It's a long adventure with memorable partners, great music and timeless cutout paper graphics. As fun as the gameplay is, it's the charming, character-driven dialogue that makes this one unforgettable.

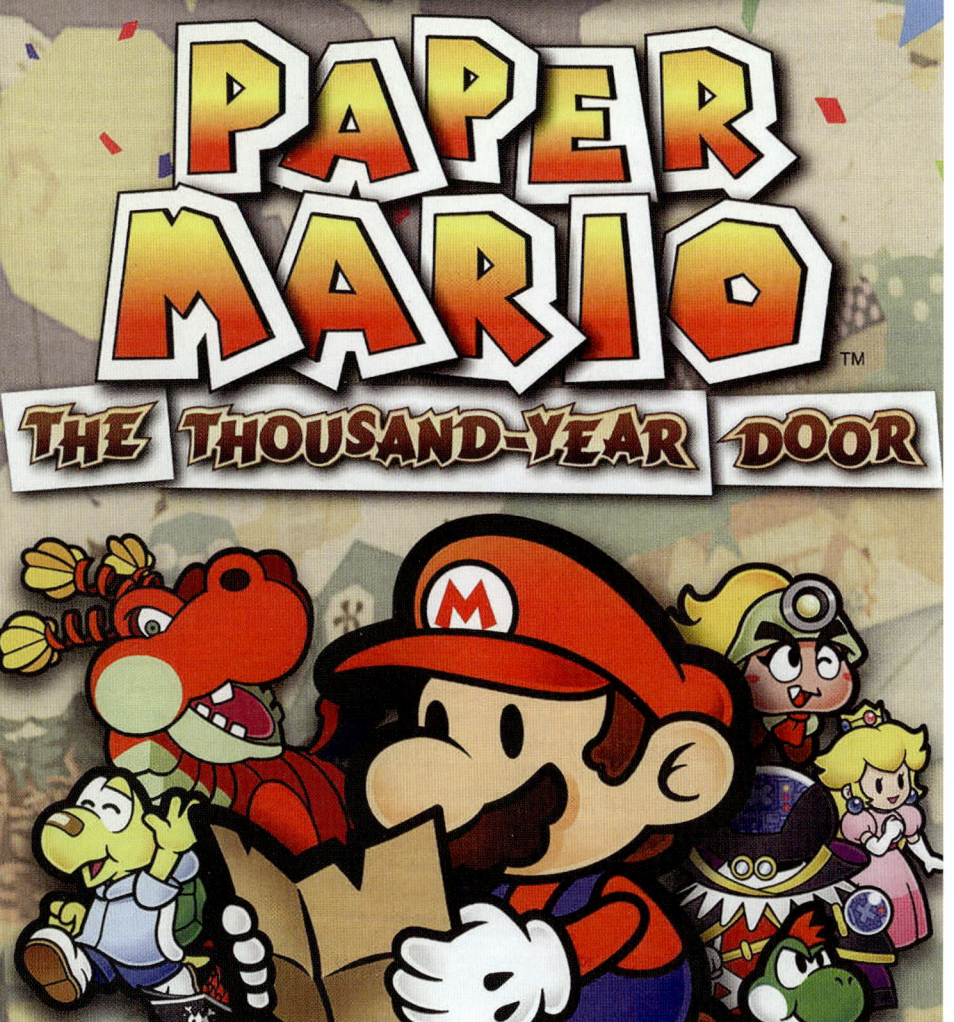

6 Super Mario 3D World + Bowser's Fury
Even in its original form on the Wii U, *Super Mario 3D World* was a ridiculously fun multiplayer platformer. Then the Switch version improved the game and added *Bowser's Fury*, a short but stunning separate campaign featuring a massive open world of obstacle courses and Kaiju fights. If Nintendo ever makes a full-length adventure based on it, it could become the new best *Mario* game.

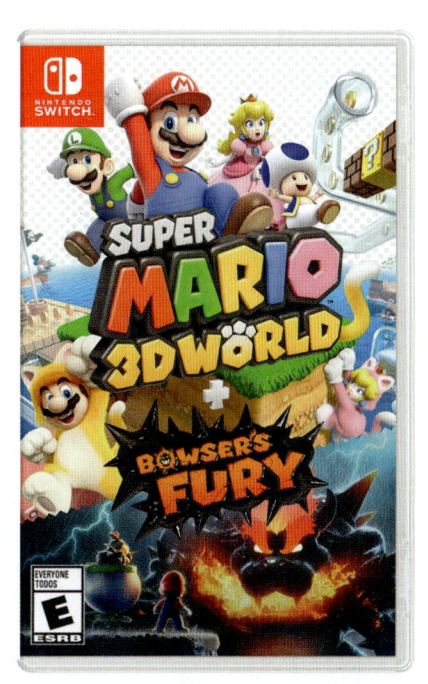

5 Super Mario 64
When *Super Mario 64* was first released in 1996, most gamers were accustomed to moving left to right. The new 3D movement was a shock to many, but those who adapted found a control scheme that felt like a carefree dance. As popular YouTube reviewer Videogamedunkey put it, "The way that Mario handles in this game is so fluid, so precise, so inherently fun and liberating that it is honestly absurd." It not only set the standard for 3D movement in video games, but it's also a joyful experience that has aged remarkably well, with a variety of challenges packed into its dense and memorable worlds.

VIDEO GAMES

4 Super Mario World
The game that introduced us to Yoshi, Cape Mario and the Super Nintendo remains one of the greatest platforming adventures ever made. *Super Mario World* is just so much fun, packed with secrets and unique enemy encounters. And the innovative overworld allowed players more freedom to forge their own path through Dinosaur Land.

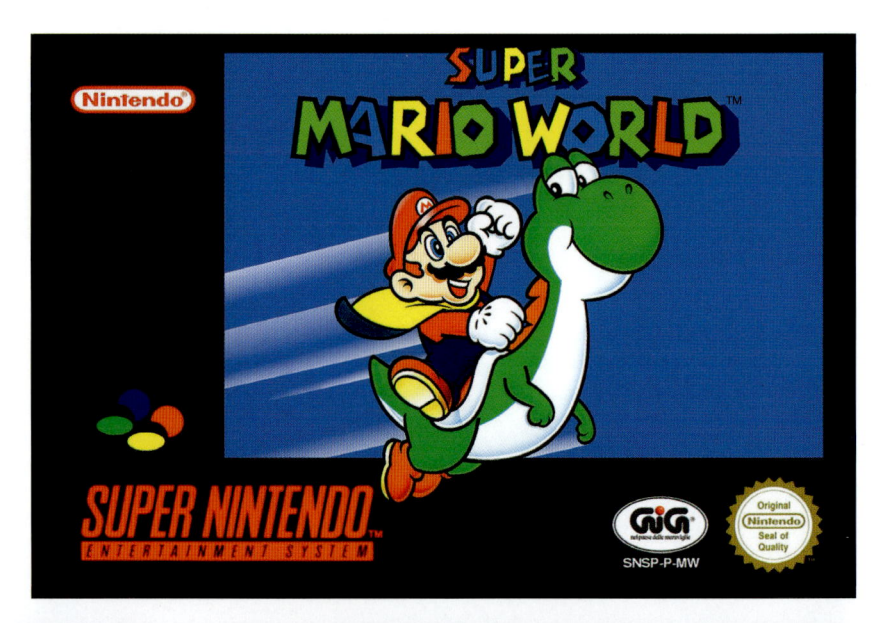

3 Super Mario Galaxy (1 and 2)
The first game introduced countless fresh ideas, including the series-defining gravity mechanic. The sequel, surprisingly changing very little, added new power-ups and brought in Yoshi. But as Tom McShea of *GameSpot* said, "It never rests on its laurels for a second, constantly presenting new objectives and mechanics to push you to never-before-seen places." You'll be happy with either of these games, but you'll only really be complete with both.

58 THE UNOFFICIAL GUIDE TO MARIO

2 *Super Mario Bros. 3*
Originally released in 1988, *Super Mario Bros. 3* is still impressive to this day. Throughout the game's 90 levels, there's a seemingly endless supply of memorable enemies, power-ups, minigames and fun platforming sections. The graphics and sound design are top-shelf, pushing the NES to its limit and even giving modern games a run for their money. This is the game where the *Mario* series truly became a universe unto itself.

> "*SMB3* is the perfect sequel. It revolutionized the way these games are played."
> THE PIXELS

> "*Odyssey* is less of a reinvention, and more of an explosion. It is a game you should play."
> DAVE THIER, *FORBES*

1 *Super Mario Odyssey*
Immaculately polished and infinitely replayable, *Super Mario Odyssey* is the crowning achievement of *Mario* platformers, if not Nintendo games—nay, video games—in general. Every single second of the game is fun. In addition to the most responsive and acrobatic *Mario* controls yet, the 17 kingdoms that make up the game are packed with challenges, Easter eggs, enemies to capture and moments of pure gaming bliss. Just when you think the adventure is over, you find that the best is yet to come. Every *Mario* game expands on those that came before, but it somehow feels like they were all building to this.

This isn't a miniature model, it's an aerial view of Super Nintendo World at Universal Studios Japan. The attention to detail is breathtaking.

| PART 3 |

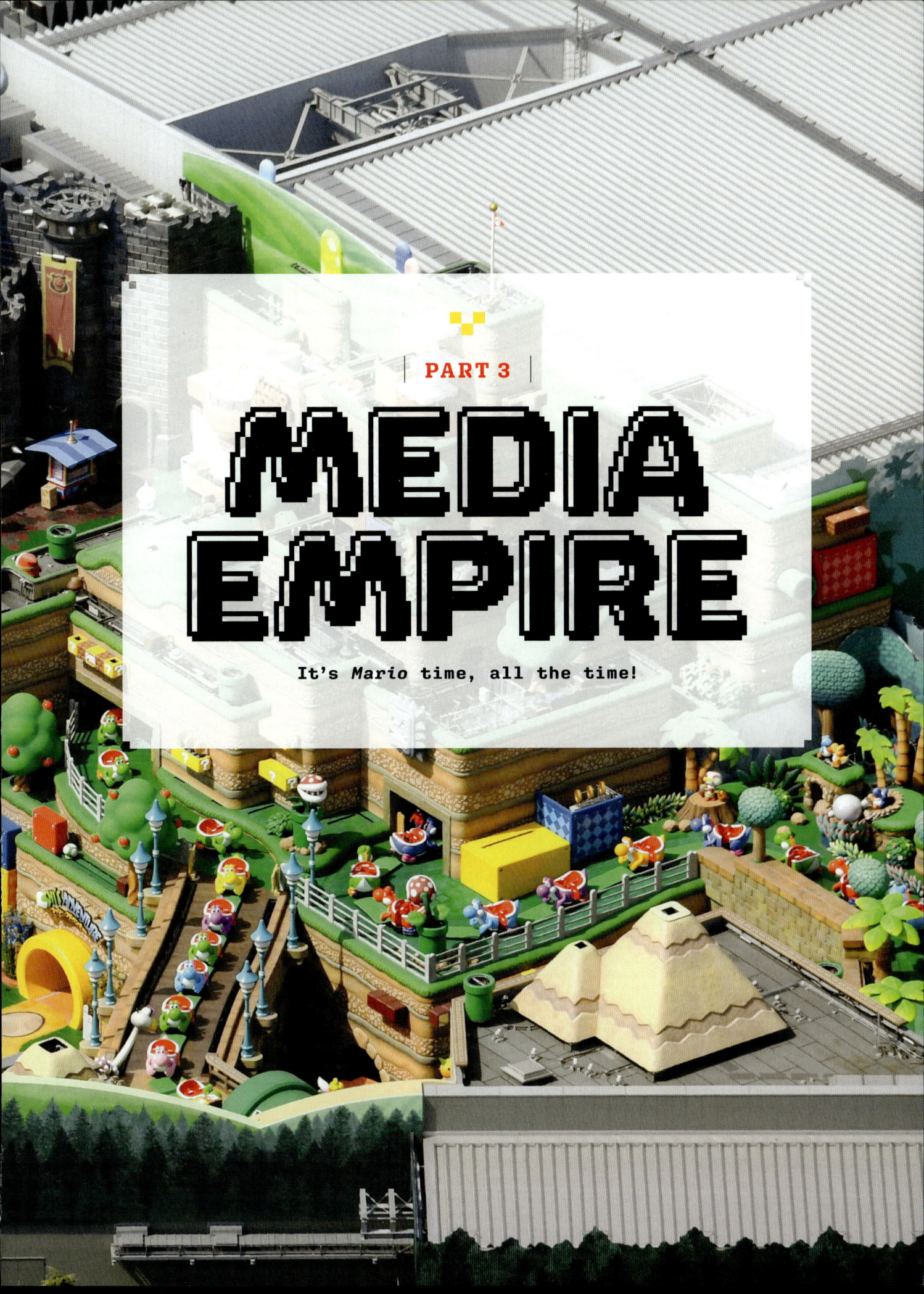

MEDIA EMPIRE

It's *Mario* time, all the time!

MEDIA EMPIRE

A NEW JUMP TO THE BIG SCREEN

Dive into all the hype and hesitance over 2023's *The Super Mario Bros. Movie*.

BY JAMES OXYER

This film, as well as Mario himself, had huge shoes to fill in the adventure ahead. No wonder he looks so nervous.

For over 20 years following the disastrous release of the live-action *Super Mario Bros.* film in 1993, the prospect of another *Mario* movie seemed bleak. But during the infamous Sony Pictures hack of 2014—in which nearly 200,000 emails were leaked to the public—readers zeroed in on a particularly interesting thread where producer Avi Arad seemed to confirm a deal between Sony and Nintendo to develop an animated film based on *Super Mario Bros.*

It would take until 2018 for Nintendo to officially announce they were working on an animated *Mario* film, but not with Sony. Instead, they were collaborating with Universal's animation division, Illumination Entertainment (*Despicable Me, The Secret Life of Pets*) to bring *Mario* to the big screen again. Producing duties would fall to Illumination founder and CEO Chris Meledandri, as well as *Mario* creator Shigeru Miyamoto. In a statement to *Variety*, Meledandri said that Miyamoto would be "front and center in the creation of [the] film." He also addressed the 1993 adaptation, saying, "I like that this was not done

CHRIS PRATT

well the first time. I think that's more exciting or more worthy than simply making another version of a film that was done incredibly well to begin with."

Behind the camera, an experienced team of creatives were tasked with bringing the *Super Mario Bros.* universe to life. Directing duties were given to Aaron Horvath and Michael Jelenic, the creators of the long-running *Teen Titans* reboot, *Teen Titans Go!* Horvath even directed the film based on the series (*Teen Titans Go! To the Movies*), while *The Super Mario Bros. Movie* marks Jelenic's directorial debut. The task of writing the script went to Matthew Fogel, who also penned Illumination's *Minions: The Rise of Gru* as well as *The Lego Movie 2* for Warner Bros.

The film follows Mario as he journeys through the Mushroom Kingdom alongside Princess Peach to rescue Luigi from Bowser, who plans on destroying the kingdom. Hollywood superstar Chris Pratt (*Guardians of the Galaxy, Jurassic World*) voices Mario, while comedic actor Charlie Day (known for *It's Always Sunny in Philadelphia*) voices his brother/sidekick, Luigi. Princess Peach is played by Anya Taylor-Joy (star of the Netflix hit *The Queen's Gambit* and the 2024 *Mad Max* film *Furiosa*), while the film's antagonists, Donkey Kong and Bowser, are voiced by Seth Rogen and Jack Black, respectively. The film also features comedic talents Keegan-Michael Key (one half of the duo Key & Peele) as Toad and Fred Armisen (*Saturday Night Live, Portlandia*) as Cranky Kong.

Movies adapted from video games have been notorious for their poor reception, both financially and critically. In recent years, video game adaptations for younger audiences have tended to fare much better than their teen/adult-oriented counterparts. A recent success story is the *Sonic the Hedgehog* movies. After a trailer reveal in 2019, fans claimed the film's character design

CHARLIE DAY

Luigi faces plenty of challenges himself in the film.

ANYA TAYLOR-JOY

> "It was always going to be necessary to reinvent Mario for him to carry a movie."
> **OLI WELSH, POLYGON**

Princess Peach (right) is feistier than ever before in the film, and her loyal assistant, Toad (left), is there to help her, as is his sacred duty.

MEDIA EMPIRE

JACK BLACK

No one has voiced any complaints about Jack Black's performance as Mario's number one foe.

for Sonic "was 'creepy' and 'upsetting'" (according to *Vulture*). The backlash resulted in the film's VFX artists completely redesigning the character. But after a rough start, the film was a box-office success and received positive reviews from critics and audiences alike, thanks to its strong script and embrace of the cartoonish elements of the premise. It even led to a sequel in 2022 featuring the voice talents of Idris Elba and spin-off TV series.

The Super Mario Bros. Movie teaser trailer debuted on October 6, 2022 to mixed reactions. Much like how Sonic's design was mocked after its first trailer release, the teaser had fans wary of an important character detail: Mario's voice. In the trailer, Pratt delivers Mario's lines in his own all-American accent. The studio seemed to take this into account with the film's second trailer, which featured a closer look at other aspects of the film, such as a visually stunning Mushroom Kingdom and a tease at a *Mario Kart* subplot.

SETH ROGEN

Like their very first appearance together, Donkey Kong and Mario face off in the film.

Toad may be deceptively adorable, but his strong heart and desire to help make him a central character.

KEEGAN-MICHAEL KEY

When *The Super Mario Bros. Movie* finally premiered in the United States on April 7, 2023, reviews were mixed. But while some viewers felt their concerns from the trailers were validated by the film, others felt many aspects lived up to the promotional hype. *IGN*'s review stated that the animation set "a very high bar," while *Nerdist* dubbed Illumination "the perfect choice to make *Mario* movies." Some of the highest praise for the film came from *Collider*, who wrote, "Jelenic, Horvath and Fogel make this feel more like a labor of love, as they've been given the keys to the (Mushroom) kingdom, and are allowed to go all-in with what any fan would want to see in a film like this." *The Super Mario Bros. Movie* even received two Golden Globe nominations: Best Animated Feature and Best Orginal Song (for the incredibly catchy "Peaches")

SPEAKING OF... THE ORIGINAL VOICE(S) OF MARIO

When you think of Mario, you might immediately imagine the now-iconic voice of actor Charles Martinet exclaiming, "It's-a me, Mario!" But believe it or not, the debut of Mario's voice was actually in a 1989 fire safety video titled *Super Mario's Fire Brigade*, with voice actor Toru Furuya voicing the character. According to *Game Rant*, "[Furuya] even voiced Mario in the first-ever movie for the character— *Super Mario Bros.: Great Mission to Rescue Princess Peach*."

And Furuya isn't alone. Before Martinet first voiced the character in 1992's *Super Mario Bros.* pinball game, five other voice actors contributed their talents in various capacities, according to *Game Rant*: "Larry Moran, Lou Albano, Walker Boone, Ronald B. Ruben and Nicholas Glaeser [...] some even in video games."

Of course, when Martinet lent his voice to the pinball game in 1992 and *Mario's Game Gallery* in 1995, Nintendo knew they had found the right man for the job. Many of Martinet's predecessors attempted a gruff Italian voice for the character. Martinet, however, felt this was too unpleasant for children and opted for a friendlier, higher-pitched timbre—a decision that eventually led him to win the Guinness World Record for "the most video game voiceover performances as the same character" (at least 100 as Mario).

MEDIA EMPIRE

TV MARIO

SUPER

The short-lived TV series becomes a cult classic among die-hard fans.

| BY JAMES OXYER |

It was the late 1980s. *G.I. Joe*, *He-Man* and other children's cartoons had taken television screens by storm. Looking for the next big hit, DiC animation head Andy Heyward met with Nintendo of America executive Howard Lincoln about teaming up. The result of this collaboration was *The Super Mario Bros. Super Show!*, and it would not be an ordinary animated program.

The show featured live-action segments following Mario and Luigi's (played by WWE Hall of Fame wrestler "Captain" Lou Albano and Danny Wells, respectively) comedic misadventures around their Brooklyn apartment, after which they would get sucked through their plumbing system into an animated Mushroom Kingdom, where cartoon versions of themselves would go on adventures with Princess Toadstool. The show also had a revolving door of live-action guest appearances, including Cyndi Lauper, Elvira, Ernie Hudson and even Magic Johnson!

Super Show premiered on Sept. 4, 1989, and achieved the "highest ever [ratings] nationally for a syndicated first-run cartoon," according to a September 1989 issue of *Broadcasting* magazine. This was not your standard cartoon but rather a unique blend of live action and animation, of sitcom and video game adventure—all showcasing some of the era's biggest pop culture figures and an amazingly '90s rap theme featuring these lyrics: "If your sink is in trouble, you can call us on the double/ We're faster than the others/ You'll be hooked on the brothers!" Unfortunately, the "Plumber Rap" has not reappeared elsewhere. ■

When they're in the "real world," Mario and Luigi live a surprisingly normal NYC life, at least compared to the world that exists in their plumbing.

66 THE UNOFFICIAL GUIDE TO MARIO

SHOW

Even in the shows, Mario is always around to save the day with the help of Toad and power-ups like the Tanooki leaf.

How would you fare in a head-to-head *Super Mario Bros.* televised competition?

A Magical (But Challenging) Misfire

Debuting in 1990 on The Children's Channel in Europe, *The Super Mario Challenge* featured kids competing against one another by playing different levels of *Super Mario Bros*. The show was hosted by Mario (played by American magician John Lenahan, the first person in 85 years to be expelled from the Magic Circle after he explained a card trick on TV).

Unfortunately, the show only lasted one season—but clips from *The Super Mario Challenge* can now be found on YouTube.

67

MEDIA EMPIRE

THE SOUNDS OF SUCCESS

Nintendo scores points for the music in its *Mario* franchise.

| BY NOAH PETRILLO |

Playing *Mario* might not be as fun, especially in the early games, without the accompanying music. The famous tune almost everyone can recognize, the tune that has come to be associated with the entire *Mario* franchise, is officially called the "Ground Theme" or "Overworld Theme." Composed by Nintendo sound designer Koji Kondo, that first song of the six heard in the original *Super Mario Bros.*, according to Kondo, took the longest to write. In an interview with *Game Maestro*, Kondo explains "Everything was composed directly on the computer, entering notes manually."

Kondo has also written themes for the *Legend of Zelda* series and has returned for most of the major *Mario* games, including *Super Mario Galaxy*, which is considered to be the best *Mario* game score of all time by *TheTopTens*. In fact, Kondo has either led or assisted in the music and sound design of nearly every single *Mario* title. He even returned to work with Brian Tyler to compose the score for *The Super Mario Bros. Movie*, released in 2023.

From iconic little songs like the "Underground Theme" (endearingly mimicked as "Denim denim denim") to the unforgettable sound effects like the "boing" of jumping, the catchy sounds of the *Mario* universe are a result of the talents of Koji Kondo.■

Music Park, found in *Mario Kart 8 Deluxe*, is a racetrack built around the series' tunes—literally.

VIRAL SENSATIONS

In a viral trend on YouTube and TikTok, musicians will play the "Overworld Theme" from the original game as it's played on a screen. The musician will break up the tune to include sound effects of jumping and collecting coins. Versions of this trend have garnered millions of views. Users have also repeated this trend with *Mario Kart*, halting the track music to shift into the Super Star power-up theme.

Tutorials such as YouTuber PianoMan333's "Best *Mario* Songs on Piano" can teach you to play the music of *Mario*!

Mario poses with Takashi Tezuka (left), Shigeru Miyamoto (center) and Koji Kondo (right) at Mario's 30th Anniversary Concert.

Can you imagine playing any *Mario* game without the accompanying music? The main theme is almost as recognizable as Mario himself!

MEDIA EMPIRE

AN A-LIST PLUMBER

Hollywood and its stars can't get enough of *Mario*.

| BY NOAH PETRILLO |

RIHANNA

Rihanna channels Daisy with unbelievable style and grace.

Mario References in Pop Culture

■ As a promotional gag, the film *Free Guy* released a poster based on *Super Mario 64*.

■ According to *This Week's Movie*, Dan Kwan, co-director of the film *Everything Everywhere All at Once*, revealed that his favorite "Easter egg"—or hidden reference in the film—is the inclusion of a sound from *Super Smash Bros.* The sound of the pinky uppercut in the film is the same as the home run bat in the video game!

■ In the hit show *Family Guy*, Mario rescues Princess Peach (as per usual), and the show makes a joke out of Mario's likely unrequited love for Peach.

70 THE UNOFFICIAL GUIDE TO **MARIO**

SETH ROGEN

LAUREN MILLER

ANYA TAYLOR-JOY

Anya Taylor-Joy, dressed as Princess Peach here, plays Peach in 2023's *The Super Mario Bros. Movie*.

Seth Rogen, who plays Donkey Kong in the 2023 film, and his wife, Lauren Miller, dressed up as Mario and Luigi for Halloween.

For the 35th anniversary of *Super Mario Bros.* in Nov. 2020, *Saturday Night Live* parodied the main cast of characters.

KENAN THOMPSON

ELON MUSK

KATE McKINNON

In the "Super Mario Rescues the Princess" episode of *Seth MacFarlane's Cavalcade of Cartoon Comedy* series, Mario asks for a kiss after rescuing Peach.

GRIMES

KYLE MOONEY

MEDIA EMPIRE

WELCOME TO SUPER NINTENDO WORLD

Live your *Mario* fantasies in real life at one of these Universal Studios amusement parks.

BY JAMES OXYER

Mascots of your favorite characters roam the parks, just waiting to interact with you and take photos.

For decades, Nintendo has sought to provide audiences with groundbreaking, imaginative experiences— a goal that led them to revolutionize the video game industry and assert themselves as a household name across the world. Their pursuit of this goal eventually led them in a bold new direction: turning their virtual worlds into a physical reality.

In 2015, Nintendo announced that they were partnering with Universal Studios to turn Super Nintendo's worlds and characters into a theme park experience, with Universal executive Tom Schroder announcing that "the immersive experiences will include major attractions at Universal's theme parks and will feature Nintendo's most famous characters and games," according to *Business Insider*.

Super Nintendo World officially opened in Universal Studios Japan in Osaka on March 18, 2021, showcasing vibrant colors, pixelated architecture and lots of familiar items and locations for fans of Nintendo games. The park is designed to feel isolated from the rest of Universal Japan, which helps to give visitors a fully immersive Nintendo experience.

Some highlights of Super Nintendo World include:

Mario Kart: Koopa's Challenge

Located inside a detailed re-creation of Bowser's castle, *Mario Kart: Koopa's Challenge* is the park's main attraction. The ambitious ride combines a normal roller coaster with an augmented reality (or "AR") video game. Visitors are given a headset to put on before entering the ride, and through the headset, they can see the ride's AR imagery. Within the AR game, you

> "There's no area inside the park that doesn't feel hand-crafted and totally convincing."
> **ROBERT SEPHAZON,**
> *VIDEO GAMES CHRONICLE*

MEDIA EMPIRE

Make sure to get a Power-Up Band (shown here) to keep track of your points and compete with friends as you explore the intricate world.

It's always a Mario party in Super Nintendo World. Universal really went all-in.

Mario Kart: Koopa's Challenge (shown here) combines the feeling of being in a real kart with Augmented Reality.

can blast competitors with turtle shells while racing through *Mario Kart* levels including Rainbow Road, Bowser's Castle, Toad's Turnpike and more.

Unlike traditional roller coasters that remain the same for decades, the use of an AR game in *Koopa's Challenge* offers the potential for an evolving experience over the coming years.

Yoshi's Adventure

While *Mario Kart* can be visually intense for some people, *Yoshi's Adventure* is intended as a more family-friendly experience. It's a slow-paced ride in which visitors travel on Yoshi's back high above the park, with the goal of spotting all the giant colored eggs laid out along the ride's path. While thrill-seekers may be disappointed with the ride's leisurely pace and simple game objective, it does offer a good chance to observe the park's impressive architecture from an exceptional vantage point.

Activities and Minigames

Despite only two major rides, the park is filled with smaller activities and minigames for fans to enjoy. These include challenges like Piranha Plant Nap Mishap, a *Mario*-themed game of whack-a-mole where the objective is to silence alarm clocks before they awaken a piranha plant, and the Bob-omb Kaboom Room, where touching hidden *Mario* logo panels causes animations of Mario and friends to appear.

To complement these activities, visitors also have the option to purchase a "Power-Up Band"— a wristband that keeps track of every virtual coin you find across the park, every activity you engage with and every attraction you ride and tallies them into achievements. You can then compete with other visitors on a virtual leaderboard.

74 THE UNOFFICIAL GUIDE TO **MARIO**

"It makes a big impression, seeing the park in real life. It feels like I've entered the real Mushroom Kingdom."
SHIGERU MIYAMOTO

Score! The Theme Park Is Now in the U.S.

American fans eager to experience Super Nintendo World for themselves don't have to buy plane tickets to Japan. Super Nintendo World recently opened in the U.S. at Universal Studios Hollywood and is expected to open in Orlando in the summer of 2025.

Super Nintendo World Hollywood features just one ride (*Mario Kart: Bowser's Challenge*), but like Super Nintendo World Japan, it has several interactive areas as well as themed shopping at the 1-UP Factory. There are also dining options, including the Toadstool Cafe, and visitors can purchase Power-Up Bands to compete with other parkgoers.

According to *TheTravel*, Orlando's park will feature three rides: *Mario Kart: Bowser's Challenge*, *Yoshi's Adventure* and *Donkey Kong's Mine Cart Madness* (by this point, the *Donkey Kong* area will also be open in Japan).

Merchandise
Fans can also find a plethora of Nintendo merchandise at the 1-UP Factory, including a huge variety of apparel, plushies, key chains, handbags, figurines, jigsaw puzzles and even several Nintendo-themed watches.

Food and Drink
The park offers several *Mario*-themed spots to grab a bite, such as Yoshi's Snack Island and Kinopio's Café. Expect to find dishes such as the Green Shell Calzone, the Power Star Chicken Curry and the Question Block Tiramisu.

The park received very good reviews across the board. *IGN* said it "brilliantly reinvents and gamifies the theme park experience," while *GAMINGbible* called it "a jaw-dropping spectacle of *Mario*-themed magic."

MEDIA EMPIRE

TRIVIA TIME

Test your knowledge with this quiz.

| BY NOAH PETRILLO |

1 Who is Mario's fraternal twin?
A | Wario
B | Peach
C | Luigi
D | Daisy

2 What is the name of Daisy's homeland?
A | Sarasaland
B | The Broccoli Kingdom
C | New York City
D | The Mushroom Kingdom

3 Where is Mario from?
A | Queens
B | Brooklyn
C | Detroit
D | Miami

4 What is Mario's day job?
A | Mechanic
B | He's unemployed
C | Cashier
D | Plumber

5 What is Mario's catchphrase?
A | It's-a me, Mario!
B | Mario time!
C | Let's-a go!
D | All of the above

6 In which game did Yoshi first appear?
A | *Super Mario Bros.*
B | *Super Mario World*
C | *Super Mario Galaxy*
D | *Super Mario Bros. 2*

7 In the first *Super Mario Bros.* game, what color were Mario's overalls?
A | Red
B | Blue
C | Yellow
D | Brown

8 What was Princess Peach's original name?
A | Princess Mushroom
B | Princess Block
C | Janet
D | Princess Toadstool

9 Which power-up gives Mario temporary invincibility?
A | Super Star
B | Mushroom
C | Red Shell
D | Blue Shell

10 Which *Mario* game came first?
A | *Super Mario Sunshine*
B | *Super Mario World*
C | *Super Mario Galaxy*
D | *Super Mario Odyssey*

11 Who is Wario's best friend?
A | Waluigi
B | Bowser
C | Bowser Jr.
D | Mario

12 In what game does Daisy first appear?
A | *Super Mario Bros.*
B | *Super Mario Bros. 2*
C | *Super Mario Land*
D | *Super Mario World*

13 What item does Dr. Mario typically throw around?
A | Fireballs
B | Pills
C | Hammers
D | Blue Shells

14 On what game system did *Mario Kart: Double Dash!!* release?
A | GameCube
B | SNES
C | Wii
D | Wii U

15 Who is Yoshi's tennis partner?
A | Birdo
B | Baby Mario
C | Toad
D | Another Yoshi

16 Which track is present in every *Mario Kart* game?
A | Wario Stadium
B | Moo Moo Meadows
C | Mario Circuit
D | Rainbow Road

ANSWER KEY: 1. C, 2. A, 3. B, 4. D, 5. D, 6. B, 7. B, 8. D, 9. A, 10. B, 11. A, 12. C, 13. B, 14. A, 15. A, 16. D

4P Versus Game Available

Nintendo has come full circle. It first scored big as an arcade game maker, then it launched its home consoles. Now, the hit home racing game *Mario Kart* is back in the arcade!

THE UNOFFICIAL GUIDE TO MARIO

Editorial Director
ANNABEL VERED

Editor-in-Chief
NOAH PETRILLO

Creative Director
JESSICA POWER

Executive Editor
JANET GIOVANELLI

Design Director
SKYE BACK

Features Editor
ALYSSA SHAFFER

Deputy Editors
RON KELLY
AMY MILLER KRAVETZ
ANNE MARIE O'CONNOR

Managing Editor
LISA CHAMBERS

Senior Art Director
PINO IMPASTATO

Art Directors
ALBERTO DIAZ
JACLYN PARRIS
NATALI SUASNAVAS
JOSEPH ULATOWSKI

Production Designer
PETER NICEBERG

Contributing Writers
JAMES OXYER
JOSEPH RAUCH
KYLE SCHMIDLIN

Senior Photo Editor
JENNY VEIGA

Photo Editor
AMY WRINKLE

Production Manager
PAUL RODINA

Copy Editor
MELISSA BRANDZEL

Production Assistants
TIANA SCHIPPA
ALYSSA SWIDERSKI

Editorial Assistants
MICHAEL FOSTER
ALEXIS ROTNICKI

a360media

President & Chief Media Officer
DOUG OLSON

EVP, Consumer Revenue
ERIC SZEGDA

Chief Content Officer
AMANDA DAMERON

EVP, Chief Revenue Officer
CAREY WITMER

SVP, Marketing
SUSAN PARKES

VP, Consumer Marketing
HOLLY OAKES
TOM MALONEY

Senior Director, Consumer Marketing
BRIAN THEVENY

Director, Consumer Marketing
MELANIE PISELLI

Circulation Manager
BILL FIAKOS

Published by A360 Media LLC. All rights reserved. Reproduction in whole or in part without prior permission of the publisher is prohibited.

PHOTO CREDITS

COVER Nintendo (13); Digital Imaging Specialist: Eric Wolslager **1** Nintendo **2-3** Andrey Armyagov/Alamy Stock Photo;Nintendo (3); Nintendo/Amazon **4-5** Nintendo **6-7** Nintendo (7) **8-9** Nintendo (3); Universal/Everett Collection; Nintendo (3) **10-11** Nintendo (5) **12-13** Staji/Alamy Stock Vector; Nintendo (8) **14-15** Nintendo (4) **16-17** Nintendo (12) **18-19** Nintendo (9) **20-21** Shutterstock/robtek **22-23** Nintendo; Shutterstock/Jarretera **24-25** Shutterstock/Kit Leong; ArcadeImages/Alamy Stock Photo; Shutterstock/robtek; Nintendo **26-27** ArcadeImages/Alamy Stock Photo; Nintendo; pumkinpie/Alamy Stock Photo; **28-29** Shutterstock/robtek; Shutterstock/Jarretera; ArcadeImages/Alamy Stock Photo; Nintendo (2) **30-31** Nintendo (3); Rauja/Shutterstock; Shutterstock/RoseStudio; Nintendo; ArcadeImages/Alamy Stock Photo **32-33** Nintendo (3); picturesbyrob/Alamy Stock Photo **34-35** Nintendo (6) **36-37** Shutterstock/robtek **38-39** Nintendo (2); Shutterstock/v74; Nintendo (2) **40-43** Judith Collins/Alamy Stock Photo; Nintendo (11) **44-45** Nintendo (5) **46-47** Nintendo (3); Shutterstock/seeshooteatrepeat **48-49** Nintendo (5); Shutterstock/v74 **50-51** Nintendo (7) **52-53** Nintendo (4) **54-55** Nintendo (2); Shutterstock/Pe3k; Shutterstock/Alla Simacheva **56-57** Nintendo (5) **58-59** Nintendo (4) **60-61** The Asahi Shimbun via Getty Images **62-63** Nintendo (2); AFF-USA/Shutterstock; Broadimage/Shutterstock; FlixPix/Alamy Stock Photo; Nintendo; Evan Agostini/Invision/AP/Shutterstock **64-65** Nintendo; People Picture/Gerome Kochan/Shutterstock; Jon Kopaloff/Getty Images; Nintendo (2); Chelsea Lauren/Shutterstock **66-67** DiC Enterprizes/Everett Collection (4); Nintendo **68-69** Nintendo; Nintendo; YouTube; AFP via Getty Images **70-71** Nintendo; David Fisher/Shutterstoc; Mediapunch/Shutterstock; Fox; VEGAN / BACKGRID; Nintendo; NBC (4) **72-73** REUTERS/Alamy Stock Photo **74-75** Yomiuri/AP Images (2); The Asahi Shimbun via Getty Images; Shutterstock/Usa-Pyon **76-77** Nintendo (5); **78-79** Shutterstock/ArliftAtoz2205

Manufactured by Topix Media Lab
14 Wall Street, Suite 3C
New York, NY 10005 USA

PRINTED IN CHINA

ISBN-13: 978-1-956403-90-9
ISBN-10: 1-956403-90-6

1C-C24-1

This publication is editorially independent and has not been licensed or approved by the owners of the characters or entertainment properties.